The Catholic Faith Explained

Michel Therrien, STL, STD

The Catholic Faith Explained

SOPHIA INSTITUTE PRESS

Manchester, New Hampshire

Sophia Institute Press
Box 5284, Manchester, NH 03108
1-800-888-9344

www.SophiaInstitute.com

Sophia Institute Press® is a registered trademark of Sophia Institute.

Paperback ISBN 978-1-64413-065-0

eBook ISBN 978-1-64413-066-7

Library of Congress Control Number: 2020932018

First printing

To my son Isaac Kolbe

So the Jews gathered around him and said to him, "How long are you going to keep us in suspense? If you are the Messiah, tell us plainly." Jesus answered them, "I told you and you do not believe. The works I do in my Father's name testify to me. But you do not believe, because you are not among my sheep. My sheep hear my voice; I know them, and they follow me. I give them eternal life, and they shall never perish. No one can take them out of my hand. My Father, who has given them to me, is greater than all, and no one can take them out of the Father's hand. The Father and I are one.... If I do not perform my Father's works, do not believe me; but if I perform them, even if you do not believe me, believe the works, so that you may realize [and understand] that the Father is in me and I am in the Father."

—John 10:24–30, 37–38

Contents

The Catholic Faith Explained

Introduction

This book is written for those curious to understand Christianity from the perspective of the Catholic Church, especially those who have been baptized and raised in the Faith as "cradle Catholics," but who have never (perhaps) understood the Faith on a personal level. Even more importantly, this book might be helpful to those who are inclined to walk away from their childhood Faith and need to understand better what they might be leaving behind. It could help those in their college years or even motivated high school students who are questioning their Faith. I can also see this book helping those inquiring into the Catholic Faith for the first time and in need of a simple but straightforward introduction to Christianity.

By calling this work an invitation to Christianity, I do not intend to present all the particulars or distinguishing facets of Catholicism. Rather, I am seeking to provide the "big picture" about what Christianity proposes to the world about who God is and why believing in Him is important to one's life. What really is the point of the Faith, after all? While this might seem like an unnecessary question, for many baptized Catholics today it is the most significant question to answer. I have met Catholics—both practicing and nonpracticing—who do not understand the big picture of their childhood Faith, nor how the pieces of Christianity fit together. It thus feels as though we live in a time when we must go back to square one and begin anew with the fundamentals, many of which are lost on the average cradle Catholic.

When I speak to parish audiences, people often say to me, "I have never heard this before," or "Why didn't anyone ever teach me this as a child?" Truthfully, if they had any religious education whatsoever as children, they probably *have* heard it before—whatever it was that I had explained—but what they hadn't heard was the overarching framework that makes all the pieces come together into a coherent, mature vision of the Christian Faith. Many Catholics pass into adulthood with a child's understanding of the beliefs and practices of Christianity. I do not mean this as a judgment, just an observation.

While this book is an invitation to Christianity, it is not overly simplistic in its presentation. I attempt to convey the true and deepest substance of Christianity, but in a manner accessible to sincerely curious adults, no matter how young. While I also attempt to be cognizant of the kinds of questions and objections people have to Christianity in today's world, I use only two sources. I support what I present with Scripture and the *Catechism of the Catholic Church*. My reason is this: I am attempting neither an argument to prove Christianity to the skeptic nor a defense of the Catholic Faith to the non-Catholic Christian. Rather, I am simply describing Christianity as the Catholic Church understands it. I do not intend this presentation to be exhaustive or to address topics meant for a later stage of formation and understanding. In other words, I do not intend any omission to suggest that what I leave out is unimportant, nor do I speculate about disputed questions. I just do not wish to get into the weeds. I am trying to remain at the level of the big picture—the principal beliefs that form the framework of Christianity—especially for those trying to understand the essential core of what the Christian religion professes to believe about the God of Jesus Christ.

I have divided the book into twenty relatively short chapters. Every chapter is its own lesson, but the later chapters do refer to prior ones and build on what I addressed previously. I have sequenced the lessons in a certain logical order, beginning with the most basic questions concerning how we come to know God and how God reveals Himself to us. Then, I look at who God is as Scripture reveals him. I end with what Christianity professes about God's plan for humanity and what it means to live as a disciple of Jesus Christ and a member of the Catholic Church—which is not simply one Christian denomination among many but the Church of Christ.

To those readers who feel they do not need this book for themselves: I hope you will find the value of having it on hand to pass along to those you meet who may be asking the kinds of questions this book attempts to answer. Yet bear in mind that faith is a gift from God. God offers this gift to everyone, but he knows that those who hear the gospel must receive the gift freely. A book like this does not prove anything to one who is not open to learning more. It provides only an opportunity to understand what faith in Jesus Christ is all about.

1

The Necessity of Faith for Life

If you think about friendships, you will notice how much they depend upon trust. In fact, when trust is broken, friendship ends quickly. Have you ever thought about what trust is and how it works? Trust is what we extend to people when we believe that what they say and do is truthful and good. In other words, we cannot trust people who lie with their words or actions or who harm us; we can trust only people who are honest. To be honest is not only to be truthful but also to be upright in our intentions, always seeking the true good of others. Trustworthiness is not simply about what a friend says or does when he or she is with us but, even more importantly, what a friend says and does when you are apart. True friends can be trusted because they never go behind your back and break trust with you.

Faith is the same as trust. To say that a person has "broken faith" or been "unfaithful" is to say that he has been untrustworthy. To have faith in someone is ultimately to say that we trust that person and entrust ourselves to her loving care. We believe that no matter what that person says or does, his words and deeds are always for our own good. Such a person is someone I can believe in and be vulnerable with, because she will treasure who I am by her actions and her words. I am safe with this person and do not need to protect myself because I trust him with my life and innermost self. This is the definition of faith, and faith is the necessary condition of any human friendship.

Human beings have a deep need for faith and friendship, without which we cannot survive. Think about what would happen in your life if you could not trust anyone about anything. How would you get through one day like that? To trust others is an essential part of being human and being happy. Yet as we know, human beings are not always trustworthy; thus, we have within us a very deep and natural desire to believe in God, to believe not only that God exists, but also that he provides for us. This is why human beings have always practiced some form of religion, which is our human way of seeking a relationship with God, in hope of finding a firm basis for our lives—a place to stand with confidence that life is good and worthwhile.

Faith and Revelation

Throughout the course of human history, however, human beings have not always agreed on the best way to form a relationship with God. Since the dawn of humankind, we have tried to find different ways to reach God and to discover His will. Ancient religions often confused God for the creatures he made, such as the sun and moon, the stars, the earth, trees and animals, and so forth. Ancient peoples thus worshiped the creatures of God, rather than God himself. Because God wished to have a relationship with us and to fulfill our desire for him, God decided to reveal himself and show us how to enter into his friendship. He did this by choosing certain people with whom to have a special friendship and through whom he wanted to reveal himself to the whole world. God's self-revelation culminated in the coming of God's divine Son, Jesus Christ, about two thousand years ago. The Bible is the book that tells the story of how God has revealed himself and his will to us. The Letter to the Hebrews eloquently summarizes this story: "In many and various ways God spoke of old to our fathers by the prophets; but in these last days he has spoken to us by a Son" (1:1–2).

The most basic truth about the Christian religion is that Christians have faith in God. Not only do Christians believe that God exists, but more importantly, they believe *in* God. That is, Christians believe that God is trustworthy and cares deeply for every person, even those who do not believe in him. In the Gospel of John, Jesus explains that he calls his disciples "friends" because he has shared the truth with them and has given himself to them in countless ways (15:15). Jesus proved by his death on the cross that he is trustworthy, the perfect friend in whom we can place our complete trust. As he himself said, "Greater love has no man than this, that a man lay down his life for his friends" (John 15:13). Jesus' sacrificial love shows us that we can entrust our deepest, most intimate selves to his loving heart.

Faith in God

Christians also believe that Jesus *is* God and that Jesus has revealed to us the fullness of God's love for and faithfulness to humanity. Christians believe not only that Jesus speaks the truth, but also that everything he does is good and for our benefit. What Jesus reveals is that God is trustworthy and that we can entrust our lives to Him. The *Catechism* states, "By faith, man submits his intellect and his will to God. With his whole being man gives his assent to God the revealer" (143). To submit means simply that through faith, man gives himself to God by believing his words and obeying his commands. In faith, we know that God is trustworthy and that his commands are for our good, because they lead us to happiness, if we obey them. The *Catechism* explains that "to obey (from the

Latin *ob-audire*, "to hear or listen to") in faith is to submit freely to the word that has been heard, because its truth is guaranteed by God, who is Truth itself" (144).

One of the first people in the Bible to have faith in God was Abraham (CCC 145–146). Abraham became the spiritual father of all the peoples of the world who would come to know God through faith, not idolatry (Rom. 4). Two things characterize Abraham's faith in God. First, Abraham had to believe that he was actually hearing God speak to him. He had to trust that the voice he heard was God's. Second, even more importantly, to prove his faith in God, Abraham had to believe what God was saying to him. Abraham had to obey God's command to leave his homeland and venture to a new and unfamiliar place God would show him in the faraway land of Canaan (Gen. 12–20).

It is easy to conclude from the story of Abraham that faith is simply blind obedience to God. God says things and we should just accept what he says, without questioning, without difficulty. Scripture paints a very different picture, however. Throughout salvation history, many biblical figures struggled to trust God, including Abraham (Gen. 16). To trust God is always a challenge for human beings. In any relationship, we desire to know some things with certainty, but simply cannot. For example, when a mother says she loves her child, the child ultimately has to believe what his mother says, because he cannot prove that her words are true. Yet the child's experience of his mother's actions reassures him that she is telling the truth. Over time, human beings learn to trust as they experience another person's faithfulness.

Thus, God does not simply tell us things; more importantly, he shows us that what he says is true by what he does on our behalf, just as he did for Abraham. Even though Abraham was not perfectly faithful all at once, God continued to walk with him. God's words help us to understand his deeds, while his deeds exemplify the meaning of his words. God did not merely promise that Abraham would inherit the land of Canaan. God helped Abraham through some difficult moments, allowing Abraham eventually to take possession of the land promised to him. God kept his word by means of his deeds and thus assured Abraham that his faith was not in vain (Gen. 20).

What is biblical faith?

The Church differentiates between the objective and subjective senses of the word *faith*. In the case of Abraham, the *objective* sense refers to what God commanded Abraham to do. The *subjective* sense refers to Abraham's willingness to believe God and obey the command he heard. God made a concrete promise to Abraham, who in turn had to entrust himself to that promise in faith, not knowing through his reason whether God's promise would be fulfilled. "Abraham thus fulfills the definition of faith in *Hebrews* 11:1: 'Faith is the assurance of things hoped for, the conviction of things not seen': 'Abraham believed God, and it was reckoned to him as righteousness.' Because he was 'strong in his faith,' Abraham became the 'father of all who believe'" (CCC 146).

Christians distinguish between the concrete beliefs the Church teaches and the act of faith by which a person believes these teachings. The content of our Faith answers the question "What does the Church believe?" The act of faith is our personal decision to accept these teachings as true and to live by them. The Church believes in what God has revealed through Sacred Scripture, especially through the life and teachings of Jesus and his apostles, as depicted in the Gospels and the Acts of the Apostles. This is what we call the *Deposit of Faith*. As the *Catechism* explains, "It is the Church that believes first, and so bears, nourishes, and sustains my faith" (168). Each person who encounters the Church's Faith can then respond by making a personal act of faith, accepting the Church's Faith as true and worthy of personal assent of mind and heart. "Believing is an act of the intellect assenting to the divine truth by command of the will moved by God through grace" (CCC 155). The Christian Faith encompasses both the *objective* and *subjective* aspects of belief.

Not with their senses but through the testimony of others do Christians believe in what God has revealed about himself. Faith is thus a gift of God's grace that every Christian receives at baptism. In this sense, we call faith a *theological* or *supernatural virtue*. Ordinarily, a virtue is a strength or power a person acquires by effort and hard work. Faith is not a virtue in this sense. It is a strength to believe in God's revelation, true, but we acquire this power through baptism, which makes the assent of faith easier for us.

The *Catechism* states, "Before this faith can be exercised, man must have the grace of God to move and assist him; he must have the interior helps of the Holy Spirit, who moves the heart and converts it to God" (153). This means simply that when a baptized person receives the gift of the Holy Spirit, he also receives the divine help he needs to believe in God's revelation, even though he did not witness the events of the Bible in person. The Holy Spirit assists the baptized to accept the Word of God as true. As we learn in the New Testament book The Acts of the Apostles, the Spirit's work begins even before a person has been baptized (19:2–7). The Holy Spirit is always leading us to believe in God.

Biblical faith and human suffering

Probably the biggest challenge to faith in God is human suffering. When someone hurts us, or when we experience disease or misfortune, we may feel that God does not care, that he is far away and inattentive to our pain. In such moments, we might be tempted to conclude that God does not love us, or even that God does not exist at all. Surely, a loving God would not let us suffer so much.

I will address the problem of pain and suffering in later chapters. For now, let me state that God respects human freedom. Sadly, people often abuse their freedom by choosing to sin. The problem of suffering goes back to the beginning of human history, when our first parents sinned (Gen. 3). For Christians, it is sin — not God — that causes suffering. It is faith in God that helps us endure and overcome suffering in the end. Despite the hardships of life, Christians believe that to attain Heaven, we must have faith in God by believing in his promises and obeying his commands. We also must persevere in faith through trials and tribulations. No matter what happens to us, it is clear that if we wish to experience God's blessings, we must believe that he is trustworthy. In the next chapter, we will consider how Christianity understands the relationship between religious faith and truth.

2

The Nature of Truth

Most people speak about truth as though it were a thing out there somewhere that we discover. From a Christian perspective, this is not exactly how we understand truth. It is more accurate to say that truth is a relationship between the mind and reality. It is almost easier to think of the word *truth* as an adjective instead of a noun. What we think in our minds about reality is true if what we think actually corresponds to what is real. If I say that a bicycle is red, but because I am colorblind, I am mistaken—the bicycle is actually blue—what I think is false. Today, we might be tempted to say, "Well, the bicycle is red to you, and blue to me." However, that would be a false statement: Why? Because the bicycle cannot be both red and blue at the same time. It must be either red or blue or neither color. Only one person can be correct—or both people must be colorblind!

When we speak about truth, we are describing *objective* reality and not merely our *subjective* opinion about something. When we say something is true, what we mean is that reality *is* the way we are describing it. For example, when a mathematician says that "two plus two equals four," he is not giving his opinion but making a claim that accurately describes the reality of this equation. Two plus two *is* four. If someone were to come along and state that "two plus two equals six," we would say that is false, or that the person has made an error. We would also say that these two people could not both be correct. Two plus two cannot be equal to four and six at the same time; that would be a contradiction.

An opinion is different from a truth claim. On the one hand, we use the word *opinion* to describe what we think about something when we have no way to verify our claim. What I say may be true, but it remains my opinion until verified. I may be of the opinion, for example, that human beings cause global warming, but I remain in that opinion until I (or someone) can prove what the causes of global warming are. If scientists *cannot* discover and prove the causes of global warming, then I can only have an opinion or a speculation about them. In this first sense of *opinion*, I can change from having an opinion to knowing the truth, if my intellect can verify in some way the truth or falsity of what I think or feel about something. The reality I am thinking about is either objectively so, or it is not.

On the other hand, and far more commonly, an *opinion* is an expression of our preferences and subjective values. For example, there is no objective basis for my claim that a blue tie is better than a red tie; I just happen to like blue ones better, so it is my opinion that blue is a better color than red. Similarly, I might prefer pop music to hip-hop music, which simply expresses my opinion about these two types of music. In the second sense of *opinion*, we are expressing a purely subjective point of view. The reality I am describing is not the object in question, but rather my perception of or feelings about that object— be it a color, a type of music, or a style of fashion.

Moral and religious truth claims are objective

What is confusing today is that people have a tendency to deny certain objective truth claims because we cannot prove them using the methodology of the hard sciences, such as physics or math. The realities about which people make these claims are not "measurable" in an empirical way or verifiable through scientific experimentation. This is especially the case when it comes to moral and religious truths. People today tend to think that such claims are a matter of subjective opinion in the second sense described above. It is a matter of subjective preference whether God exists, it is a subjective point of view that premarital sex is immoral, and so forth.

The problem with this kind of reasoning is that it applies the second sense of *opinion* to something that is not actually a matter of personal preference or feeling. God's existence does not depend on how I feel about him or what I subjectively prefer—as if we could truthfully state that God exists for you, but not for me. Objectively speaking, either God exists or he does not. Either premarital sex is morally good, or it is morally wrong. It cannot be good for you but bad for me at the same time. That would be a contradiction.

It is true that a person may only hold an opinion about such matters in the first sense of *opinion* I described above. That is, one may not be able to verify for himself whether God exists, or one may not grasp a moral truth on his own—and so would hold an opinion on the matter in the first sense. Nevertheless, these matters are never a matter of personal preference or feeling in the second sense of *opinion*.

How do we know what is true?

How, then, do we know that what we think actually corresponds to what is real? When what we think with our mind corresponds to what is real, we say that we know something, or we have knowledge. How do we make that correspondence happen? The answer to this question is that we come to truth in a variety of ways. One of the most obvious ways is through study. We have to study and inquire into the nature of things, in order to acquire knowledge. In the most general way, we call the process of investigation into reality *science*. Since we can study many different kinds of things, there are many different sciences. History is the study of past events. Biology is the study of organic life. Math is the study of numbers, ratio, and proportion. And so forth—you get the idea.

Each science has its own method and criteria of verifying its conclusions, but in general, we test our hypotheses and validate our claims about reality through arguments and evidence. When the evidence supports our theory, we say that we have acquired knowledge of the reality we are attempting to understand. What complicates our desire to understand reality is that many of the things we wish to know are not sensible realities. A sensible reality, or thing, is something we can grasp with one of our five senses (sight, touch, taste, hearing, and smell). Even a star a billion light years away is a sensible thing with the help of a telescope, which simply enhances our power of sight. Yet we also desire to know things our senses cannot apprehend.

What we call the *scientific method*—the process of investigation scientists use in physics, biology, and chemistry—is not the only method by which we arrive at the truth about reality. What we call *empirical methods* of science measure and evaluate only sensible objects, but—and this is critical—we also come to truth by other means, especially when what we desire to know is not empirically verifiable. One such way is through witness or testimony, as in a court of law. In fact, most of what we "know" is the result of trusting in the credible testimony of someone else who, by his witness, can verify a claim. For example, we know that a man landed on the moon, even though we were not there to see it for ourselves. We trust that the footage of Neil Armstrong's landing is real, not fraudulent. More importantly, we trust the testimony of Neil Armstrong himself.

The Nature of Truth

By means of logic, we can *reason* to truth. For example, I may apply what we call *inductive reasoning* to conclude that my child is stealing cookies. I notice that the supply is dwindling and that there are crumbs on his bed and a small smudge of chocolate on the corner of his mouth. Even though I never saw him take the cookies, from these little pieces of evidence, I reason to a conclusion. Should he admit that he did steal the cookies, he would only be verifying what I had already truthfully concluded from my observations.

Another pathway to truth is through our emotional intelligence. We can grasp certain realities accurately on an emotional level. Interestingly, our intestinal tract contains its own nervous system, giving scientists strong reason to suggest that we do "think" with our gut. There is still much to learn, but in any case, the "heart" or "gut" is also a source of "knowing" truth. Another name for this is *intuition*. More poetically, we may speak about knowing something in our hearts. One clarification I would make is that feelings can mislead us. While feelings are a pathway to truth — think of a mother's intuition, for example — they are not infallible. Our feelings can misrepresent reality and lead us into error; thus, we always must be discerning with our feelings or gut instincts.

Another way of coming to truth is by accepting the authority of another person. This requires a great deal of trust, but trustworthy authorities are great resources for knowing the truth. The best example of this is that of a loving parent. A parent often teaches her children things about life that they cannot yet figure out on their own. The children simply have to trust the authority of their father or mother, that what they say is true. As the children mature, their studies, experiences, and observations can further validate their parents' wisdom.

The point here is that we come to truth — a correspondence between the mind and reality — in a variety of ways. In truth, our grasp of reality is the result of a convergence of all the various ways we are able to perceive reality. To single out only one path to truth is a certain way to arrive at a distorted view of reality. In fact, this is how we most often fall into error. We need all the means by which reality makes itself intelligible to our minds, including the truth that comes from faith in God. Another problem with relying on only one source of truth—for example, the scientific method alone—is that it would paralyze us if we had to verify empirically every fact ourselves. How would we function? Think for a moment how the various pathways of truth help us just to get into an automobile and drive to school each day.

Philosophy and the knowledge of God

Throughout human history, philosophy has been one of the most important sciences for coming to the knowledge of truth. *Philosophy* literally means "love of wisdom." It is a science, but one quite different from the other sciences mentioned above. Philosophy uses argumentation and logic to prove or demonstrate the truth of what we might call *immaterial* or *invisible* realities, things not directly discernible to the human senses. Take, for example, things such as friendship, love, consciousness, thought, or the nature of being. We cannot put these things under a microscope or measure them, but they are no less real on this account. The moral character of human actions is also a matter of philosophy. We call *ethics* the study of human nature and what leads to human happiness or misery.

One of the most important subjects of philosophy over the centuries has been God. We call the philosophical study of God *natural theology* (from the Greek *theo-logia*, meaning "study of God"). It is natural because it does not depend upon God's special revelation, but upon reason alone. In the same way that we can explore topics such as friendship and love, we can learn about God through study, even though God is not a sensible being. How does this work?

In the first place, human beings have a natural desire to know God. We want to know where we came from and where we will end up after death. This is why the Church says, "The desire for God is written in the human heart, because man is created by God and for God; and God never ceases to draw man to himself" (CCC 27). We could say that this is a natural law of our existence—human beings desire to know God. We are, by nature, religious beings, or beings who seek to know the ultimate cause of our existence. This is something other animals do not do.

Although we humans have always worshiped God and debated our ideas about him, we have not always agreed on whether we can prove his existence. Some people think that belief in God is just a matter of subjective opinion and personal experience, and not something we can know by reason. The Church states, however, that "created in God's image ... the person who seeks God discovers certain ways of coming to know him" (CCC 31). If this is true, what can we know about God, and how do we come to this knowledge?

These are good questions that are difficult, but not impossible, to answer. The Church teaches that through human reason, by certain kinds of evidence and argumentation, we can know that God exists and what he is like. The *Catechism* explains, "These [ways of knowing God] are also called proofs for the existence of God, not in the sense of proofs in the natural sciences, but rather in the sense of 'converging and convincing arguments,' which allow us to attain certainty about the truth" (CCC 31).

Can we know that God exists?

We must use philosophical reasoning and logic to prove God's existence; furthermore, we have to begin with truths we know from other sciences. Paul makes this point in his Letter to the Romans: "For what can be known about God is plain ... because God has shown it to them. Ever since the creation of the world his invisible nature, namely, his eternal power and deity, has been clearly perceived in the things that have been made" (1:19–20). While we can never know some things about God unless he reveals them to us, some things we *can* know about him apart from his self-revelation. We will discuss in more detail God's revelation of himself in a later chapter. For now, let us turn our attention to *how* we can know through reason that God exists. To begin, we can know that God exists by reasoning from simple observations of the things we can perceive in creation, to the deeper causes behind what we observe. The approach here is to reason from what is nearer to us in our perceptions to what is more distant and abstract.

In a later chapter, we will look at some formal philosophical proofs for God's existence. In the meantime, let us consider a couple of philosophical approaches we can take to examine the question of God's existence. The philosophical question we might first ask is, "Where did everything come from?" We can trace things back in time through chains of causality. Yet because we can think infinitely about the past, by imagining one cause before another, what happens when we do this is that we never ultimately figure out how the universe began in the first place. We call this the problem of *infinite regress*. Something that is infinite has no limits, such as a beginning or an end. The infinite regress, or "going backwards" of causality is an answer that really is no answer at all, because it never explains how things got here in the first place. A finite thing (something with definite limits) like the universe cannot also be eternal or last forever. That would be a logical contradiction.

So we have to ask further why there is a universe to begin with. From a philosophical perspective, we can reason that for there to be anything at all, there must be something that started everything. If this first cause or first being were not absolute in its existence (eternal), there would just be nothing, and we would not be here.

Nothingness cannot have caused the universe to come into existence. While we have no idea what that first being is, we can grasp philosophically that such a being has to exist—some being that exists and never changes (is unmoved). The name philosophers have given to this being is *God*.

A second approach to philosophizing about God's existence is to observe the order and intelligibility of the universe. For something to be intelligible means that to some extent, it is understandable, that we are capable of examining its various parts and making sense of it. Imagine for a moment that you were walking through the desert and happened upon a laptop computer. Would you conclude that this laptop is a random event? The evidence that this cannot be the case is the order and intelligibility of a computer. The desert winds would never randomly assemble a computer out of sand. A *person* did that, and a *person* left the computer there in that place. When one ponders the complexity and order of the entire cosmos—and its beauty—it is like coming across that laptop computer. The existence of the cosmos cannot be a random event that emerges out of nothing (on its own).

When faced with the great intelligibility of the entire universe, it does not make logical sense for a Christian to conclude that God does not exist. To the contrary, the universe is one great sign of intelligence! Even though we have proven the big bang, the big question is, what caused that? In other words, if there is something intelligible, then some intelligence must have created it. If there is a universe so ordered and beautiful, it is far more logical to conclude that someone designed it and made it that way than to conclude that such a magnificent spectacle is a random event. The assertion that something as amazing as the cosmos just accidentally emerged into existence is actually quite an absurd claim. It is perhaps even a dishonest claim, motivated, perhaps, by intentions other than trying to explain the origins of everything.

The Catholic Faith Explained

As a science of reasoning, philosophy is very useful for understanding those things that are not discernable to our senses. Nevertheless, human beings are not, and never have been, satisfied with simply knowing *that* God exists. We want to know God personally—at least, we have always wanted to know something about our Creator. This is why we are quite naturally spiritual and religious beings. To deny this is like saying it's good enough to know *that* you have a friend, without actually knowing anything about that friend. Humankind has always desired to know God, and we have struggled from the beginning in our religious attempts to get to him. The problem is that we can only know who God is if God reveals himself to us. The Church teaches that God shows us who he is in two different ways. The first way is through what he has created. This is what we call natural revelation. The second is through special revelation, which refers to the ways God has communicated directly with or through actual human beings. We will explore special revelation in later chapters.

Whether God exists or not is deeply consequential to our lives. To say that God's existence is just a matter of subjective opinion or personal preference is to trivialize the single most important question with which great philosophers (and nearly every human being) have wrestled over the centuries. Even more importantly, we cannot silence humanity's endless desire to know who God is. This desire for God is essential to being human, and it matters terribly that we know the truth. Some of the greatest evils ever perpetrated have resulted from false images of God or the outright denial of his existence. Yet the greatest and most wonderful acts of love and mercy have resulted from true faith in God and knowledge of his existence and purpose. This is why faith is so important to human flourishing.

3

Christian Faith and Modern Science

Up to this point, we have discussed the different ways of coming to the knowledge of truth, including the truth about God. We saw that faith is a pathway to truth, especially insofar as we have good reasons to believe in what God has revealed through natural and special revelation. However, is it ever the case that a truth of faith seems to contradict a truth of science, such as physics or history? This *can* happen, but we must keep in mind that we can always find a way to reconcile these conflicts. Christians believe that all truth originates from one source, which is God, so while it might seem as though there are contradictions, in fact, we will find perfect symmetry between the truths of science and those religious truths originating in divine revelation, but only if we are disciplined and careful in our intellectual inquiries.

The reason the Church teaches that the truths of reason and faith can never actually contradict each other is because all things proceed from the same Divine Intelligence, who is Truth itself. What this means is that everything exists as it does because God is the master architect of all that is. Nothing can exist in one way from one point of view and exist in a completely different way from a different point of view. The difference of perceptions happens within the limited perspective of the human mind. No person has a complete view of reality, so any valid truth claim is only a partial representation of reality. This is perhaps one of the greatest contributions Einstein's theory of relativity has made to human science. It is also possible that our perceptions of reality are inaccurate and in need of revision. Over time, if we are disciplined and intellectually honest, our collective grasp of reality does improve, and our knowledge grows.

Truth and method

The Church believes that a number of principles must guide one's pursuit of truth. The first and most important principle is that one must always respect the proper scope and method of any science. For example, one should never use the science of theology to explain physics. Nor should one rely on physics to explain religious truth. Likewise, one should not use philosophy to explain biological processes, nor biology to make philosophical claims. For example, the biological law of natural selection or "survival of the fittest" does not apply to the relationships that humans must have with each other. This mistaken application of biology can support racist attitudes toward minority groups. While each method might provide some unique perspective for understanding reality, one should never conflate methods of inquiry. Another famous example of this first principle was on display during a major contention in the sixteenth and seventeenth centuries, when the Catholic scientists Copernicus and Galileo were exploring the configuration of our solar system.

At the heart of the conflict in the Galileo affair was the book of Genesis, particularly the creation narratives contained it its first three chapters. During the centuries prior to the Scientific Revolution, the Church simply assumed that Scripture provided an accurate account of the origins of the world. In those days, people believed Genesis 1–3 was scientifically reliable, for the most part.

(As an aside, medieval Christians did not believe the world was flat, as attested by Thomas Aquinas himself in the thirteenth century.) When scientists such as Copernicus and Galileo discovered that astronomy was arriving at a different picture of things than what Genesis was purported to have meant, it created a crisis within the Church.

The solution to the crisis was to see that the new scientific methods opened up new spheres of knowledge, that we must not fear such scientific advances, and that scientists could not use the scientific method to explain the truth about other aspects of reality. In the case of Genesis, the Church has clearly come to understand that "from a literary standpoint ... the inspired authors have placed [the creation narratives] at the beginning of Scripture to express in their solemn language the truths of creation—its origin and its end in God, its order and goodness, the vocation of man, and finally the drama of sin and the hope of salvation" (CCC 289). These texts do not explain the physics, chemistry, or even the age of the universe, or of humankind. This was not the intention of the author. The truths spoken of in Genesis are philosophical and theological in nature.

In those days, however, it was a mistaken application of Scripture to insist that the earth was at the center of the solar system, when the scientific evidence had begun to show that this was not the case. However—and this is why there was so much controversy over Galileo—it was also false of Galileo to claim, on the basis of his astronomical observations, that Scripture was erroneous for placing man at the center of creation. What got Galileo in trouble was the fact that he was making philosophical and theological claims about humankind and about Scripture on the basis of his astronomy. This is why the Church objected to his protests. His science was acceptable, according to the Church, but the overreach of his claim that Scripture was unreliable, and that humankind was cosmically insignificant, was unacceptable. The Church needed more time to study these new discoveries in order to reconcile the apparent discrepancies of truth claims.[1]

We now understand that no contradiction exists whatsoever between science and Scripture regarding the beginning of the cosmos. From the perspective of faith, it does not matter when or how the universe came to be, from the standpoint of physics. From Scripture, we know that God created the world and gave it a certain order, hierarchy, and value, and that humankind enjoys a special dignity among all the creatures on earth. We also know that moral evil originates from the abuse of freedom and the violation of basic moral principles written on the human heart. From physics, we know that the universe came to be through a large explosion of mass that spread out across space, forming stars, planets, and eventually the earth, on which all life, including our own, began. Both faith and reason have something important to contribute to our understanding of our origins. Both sets of truth claims actually complement one another.

Reconciling faith and reason

The second principle we have to keep in mind is that when we find an apparent contradiction of truth claims between faith and science, only one of three things is possible: (1) our science is erroneous, (2) our theological understanding of the Faith is erroneous, or (3) both the science and the theology are erroneous. To continue with our theme of origins, another point of controversy has been Darwin's theory of evolution. When Darwin first presented his

---

[1] A good scholarly source to read further about this is Annibale Fantoli's book *Galileo, for Copernicanism and for the Church*, 2nd ed. (Tucson: Vatican Observatory Publications, 1994).

theory, Genesis seemed (again) to be only a myth, which scientists had refuted. In particular, some evolutionary biologists postulated that humankind had originated from multiple original couples and locations across the earth. During the 1950s, Pope Pius XII quite boldly refuted this claim, which we call *polygenism*, by reaffirming the theological truth that all *Homo sapiens* descended from one original couple.[2] This created another crisis, even for many Catholic scientists!

Since then, geneticists have been able to show (for the most part) that all modern *Homo sapiens* do in fact descend from an original set of parents. Most anthropologists think our first parents existed somewhere between one hundred thousand and two hundred thousand years ago. This is an example where science was initially mistaken but was eventually able to prove that the teachings of faith had been correct all along. Due to her doctrine of Original Sin, which maintains that a single first couple — our first parents — committed the first sin, the Church had to insist upon the truth of *monogenism* (a single point of origin for humanity). However, not all the claims made by people of faith were entirely correct, because it seems that humankind has been alive for much longer than the biblical narrative suggests.[3]

As long as we are able to understand what the biblical authors intended to convey and what they did not, it is difficult to find actual discrepancies between the truths (or claims) of modern science and the truths of the Christian Faith. However, such discrepancies can still occur when some Christian groups insist on taking the Bible too literally in all of its details, or when scientists

[2] Pope Pius XII, encyclical letter *Humani generis* (On Certain False Opinions Which Would Threaten to Undermine the Foundations of Catholic Doctrine) (August 12, 1950).

[3] See *Wikipedia*'s article on recent African origin of modern humans for more information.

insist that the Bible contains no objective truth whatsoever. The error of religious or scientific fundamentalism occurs when people maintain convictions contrary to what the human mind demonstrates beyond a reasonable doubt.

For example, some Christians still maintain that God created the world in six twenty-four-hour days. Instead of reading the Scriptures in a proper theological manner, biblical fundamentalists will hold to their convictions in the face of evidence that proves the contrary. When this happens, it is always a situation where people are insisting upon something not in any way necessary to salvation. In the example we just considered, our salvation does not depend upon believing that God created the world in six days or over millions of years. It does not matter at all either way. The biblical authors had no scientific knowledge of anthropology, nor did they intend to explain the origins of the universe in a scientific manner.

Scientists can also be fundamentalist when they insist that religious or philosophical truth does not exist and that science explains everything. We call this distortion of the hard sciences *scientism* or *scientific positivism*. For example, the famous physicist Richard Dawkins claimed that physics proves we can explain the origins of the cosmos without God. To insist that God cannot exist is an example of scientific fundamentalism, because scientists are mistakenly claiming to have a complete explanation of the origins of the cosmos. Theories of physics cannot prove whether God exists or not. To discover that the universe is billions of years old does not disprove that God created the universe and gave it a definite purpose. Science does not make religious truth irrelevant—or vice versa.

The problem of scientific reductionism

The third and final principle that must guide how one understands the relationship between science and faith is that we may never reduce the scope of truth to that of only one science or methodology. Recall from the last chapter how we can attain truth in multiple ways—through research, philosophical argumentation, the witness of another person, intuition, and so forth. At times, people attempt to limit the scope of truth only to what they can verify by means of one method. This mostly happens when certain scholars assume that truth only pertains to claims made by their particular field of study. For example, some philosophers today insist that the only way we can understand social relations is through the writings of Karl Marx, Charles Darwin, or Sigmund Freud. While each method can provide perspective and insight, no one theory explains everything.

In a similar manner, thinkers can often exude an unjustified confidence in their view of reality. This can happen even within the confines of a given scientific discipline. When Newton's laws of motion were the main paradigm of physics, no one could imagine the revolution of quantum theory, whereby the Newtonian laws of physics became untenable when carefully observed. Truthfully, reality is very complex and difficult to understand. Our theories about things change all the time. Some of the theories we posit are just that—theories. We have never been able to prove them. Other theories become demonstrable fact over time. The key to our acquisition of knowledge, therefore, is to assume an attitude of complete humility before the mysteries of reality and of the God who created everything. To observe the world and to contemplate the existence of God with sufficient openness and awe before all we do not understand, and never will be able to understand completely, is essential for the attainment of truth. Pride can easily blind us to the truth.

The historical truth of Scripture

One last area of contention between reason and faith involves the discipline of history. The science of history has also developed in recent centuries, and new technologies and extensive research have produced a clearer picture of past events. While history is not a hard science, it does employ its own legitimate methods of inquiry. What makes history different is that it studies what philosophers call *contingent reality*. That is a fancy way to say that historians attempt to reconstruct events, motivations, and chains of social causality originating in the interplay of human freedom. Because what motivates human action is often quite hidden from view, and because memory can become distorted easily, arriving at an accurate and complete historical picture of the past is quite difficult. This is why we can read multiple "histories" of the same event, all of which differ to some degree, and all of which give us access to different dimensions of the past.

The same is true of the historical accounts recorded in Scripture. Biblical scholars are always doing their best to examine biblical history using the text of Scripture as well as evidence found outside the text. One of the discoveries biblical scholars have made is that Scripture contains multiple narratives of the same events. These histories differ in certain ways, because they reflect the perspectives of the different historians. However, careful study shows that the varying accounts do not actually contradict each other. The most obvious example of this is found in the Gospels. Each account provides a different perspective of the life of Jesus, and each conveys the truth. Where discrepancies seem to exist, honest scholarship has been able to reconcile the Gospel narratives.

What might confuse historians is the fact that the biblical authors wrote their histories from the perspective of their faith in God's involvement in the world. Some nonreligious historians might assume that this makes the historical value of Scripture obsolete. However, the Church teaches us that the faith of the biblical authors simply helps us grasp the deeper significance of the events recounted in Scripture. It is mistaken to assume that faith renders the historical account mere fiction. One fascinating example of this is the biblical account for the destruction of Sodom and Gomorrah.

The biblical narrative recounts how God caused fire and sulfur to rain down upon these two cities, utterly annihilating them as punishment for their sexual debauchery. Recently, forensic scientists have been able to conclude that an asteroid exploded just over the two cities, causing a scorching inferno to rain from the sky. This explosion caused the atmospheric temperature to rise almost instantly to 10,000 degrees Fahrenheit. Yes, the people all died instantly, too, literally becoming a glass-like substance. True story! The religious perspective of the biblical account does not delegitimize the history; it simply interprets the meaning of the events, in this case judging the destruction of Sodom and Gomorrah to be God's punishment for their iniquity. The truth of that interpretation is a matter of faith in the authority of Scripture as God's Word and is not something science can prove or disprove. I will address the authority of Scripture later.

The most controversial aspect of Scripture from a historical and generally scientific point of view is the recounting of miracles. Some modern historians and scientists simply assume that these miraculous occurrences did not happen, because these modern scholars are of the subjective opinion that such events *cannot* happen. Miraculous occurrences, however, are an integral part of human experience, even to this day. Every canonized saint of the Church has to have three miracles validated by an outside board of examiners. Just because a person has not been a direct witness to a miracle, it does not follow that miracles never occur. Such an assertion is actually a logical fallacy. In any case, one of the most essential values of Sacred Scripture is that it recounts some of the most spectacular miracles God has performed for the salvation of the human race. This is the point of Scripture—to provide a witness to God's continual presence and activity among us, despite human pride and spiritual blindness.

Despite our pride, and perhaps because of it, human beings seem to have an insatiable desire for truth. We are never content with what we presently know. Our minds continue to seek all there is to know. Overall, this is a good thing, and God actually desires that we seek to know the truth about everything. Yet we must do so with a realistic estimation of what we can and cannot comprehend. Pope St. John Paul II once stated that this "desire for knowledge is so great and it works in such a way that the human heart, despite its experience of insurmountable limitation, yearns for the infinite riches which lie beyond, knowing that there is to be found the satisfying answer to every question as yet unanswered."[4] Pope John Paul II was a great champion of science, philosophy, and theology. He famously stated that "faith and reason are like two wings on which the human spirit rises to the contemplation of truth; and God has placed in the human heart a desire to know the truth—in a word, to know himself—so that, by knowing and loving God, men and women may also come to the fullness of truth about themselves."[5]

For Christians, faith and reason complement each other and give us access to different aspects of reality. The Church does not limit herself to either faith or reason but remains open always to purifying our notions of God and reality. We cannot satisfy our desire for knowledge unless we remain open to all the avenues by which God leads us to truth. The Church summarizes the harmony between faith and science in this way:

> Though faith is above reason, there can never be any real discrepancy between faith and reason. Since the same God who

---

[4] Pope John Paul II, encyclical letter *Fides et ratio* (Faith and Reason) (September 14, 1998), no. 17.

[5] Ibid., Blessing.

reveals mysteries and infuses faith has bestowed the light of reason on the human mind, God cannot deny himself, nor can truth ever contradict truth. Consequently, methodical research in all branches of knowledge, provided it is carried out in a truly scientific manner and does not override moral laws, can never conflict with the faith, because the things of the world and the things of faith derive from the same God. The humble and persevering investigator of the secrets of nature is being led, as it were, by the hand of God in spite of himself, for it is God, the conserver of all things, who made them what they are. (CCC 159)

Most people do not realize that the Church created the modern university system and that some of the greatest scientific discoveries of all time have been made by Catholic priests and laymen. The Church even has an academy in Rome — the Pontifical Academy of Sciences — dedicated to the human sciences. The Christian Faith is open to all knowledge and will always encourage the pursuit of truth wherever we can discover it.

4

How God Reveals Himself

To summarize what we have considered thus far, Christians believe that human beings have a natural desire for God and that, by different ways, we can come to know he exists. Philosophical reasoning can help us know some things about God, but it does not reveal how best to relate to him as creatures designed for authentic spiritual and religious practice. Yet as we learn from Scripture, God desires to have a relationship with every person he creates. The primary way we have that relationship is through the gift of faith. If we rely on reason alone, we do not easily come to knowledge of true (or authentic) religious practice. Much less are we able to grasp the ultimate meaning and purpose of human existence, which is union with God. The faith that Christians have is rooted in God's revelation. Revelation is just another way of saying that God has shared with us who he is and what his purpose is for our lives.

Now that we have considered all the ways Christians believe a human being can know God through faith and reason, the next step is to understand better how God makes himself known to us. How exactly does God reveal himself? According to the Church's teaching, God's revelation happens in two ways. The first way is through what we call natural revelation; the second way is through what we call special revelation, which Sacred Scripture has preserved for us.

The Catholic Faith Explained

Recall how earlier, I described God as an artist whose intelligence is reflected in the intelligibility of creation. If we think of God with a slightly different metaphor, as a master builder, he must have had a blueprint in mind when designing and creating everything. The Church describes that master plan as the product of God's wisdom. By his wisdom, he orders all things well and aright. That wisdom is the Divine Word—*Logos* in Greek—the same Eternal Word that Christians believe became human in Jesus Christ. We will discuss this claim later on, but let us continue.

Through the Eternal Word, God created all things, meaning that every creature bears a certain likeness to that Word. Everything God makes reflects divine wisdom, bearing a certain similarity to it. As the *Catechism* says, "All creatures bear a certain resemblance to God, most especially man, created in the image and likeness of God. The manifold perfections of creatures—their truth, their goodness, their beauty—all reflect the infinite perfection of God" (41). Just as with an architect, a relationship exists between the creative mind of the architect, the blueprint for the house, and the actual house to be built, so too does a relationship exist between God's creative mind, the blueprint for creation, and the actual creation that God made.

This is especially true when it comes to the human person. A relationship exists between the Divine Mind, the first man (Adam), and the blueprint after which God made Adam. This blueprint is the Word made flesh, Jesus Christ. In his Letter to the Colossians, St. Paul says of Christ, "He is the image of the invisible God, *the first-born of all creation*; for in him all things were created, in heaven and on earth, visible and invisible, whether thrones or dominions or principalities or authorities—all things were created through him and for him. He is before all things, and in him all things hold together" (1:15–17, emphasis mine). Thus, through special revelation, preserved for us in Scripture, we come to know Jesus Christ, who is the fullness of God's revelation to the human race.

The two books of God's Word

Because every creature God has made reflects the Divine Word in some way, we can learn a great deal about the mind of God by studying what the creative mind of God has actually created. In fact, all of creation serves as a kind of analogy by which we can learn something about God; as the *Catechism* says, "Consequently, we can name God by taking his creatures' perfections as our starting point" (41). The book of Wisdom states, "For from the greatness and beauty of created things comes a corresponding perception of their Creator" (13:5). The Fathers of the Church thus spoke about the two books of God's Word—the book of nature and the book of Scripture. We need to "read" both books to get a complete picture of God and to understand the purposes of his will.

One example of a truth we learn from natural revelation is that God is almighty, or all-powerful. By observing the various forms of power in creation, we can learn something about God's power. Take the birth of a star. This process is stunningly beautiful, and it results in the conditions for the possibility of life. From this, we can conclude that God's power leads to life, not mere destruction. It also takes a long time, so God in his might is also very patient! He does not hurry or force things by his power. Rather, he allows all creatures to possess within themselves the principles of their own vitality, thereby sharing in his power. The laws of physics, which God designed and established, give rise to the stars, which are condensed by gravity to form these beautiful luminaries in the night sky—billions and billions of them. From the sheer numbers of stars, we learn also that in his almighty power, God is abundantly generous and fruitful, for he seems always to create far more than is needed.

Another even more profound way that God makes himself knowable is by having created the human person with a rational soul. The soul is not only the seat of our intellect, by which we come to knowledge. The soul is also something we can contemplate in itself, allowing us, by way of analogy, to learn something about God himself. As the *Catechism* describes it: "The *human person*: with his openness to truth and beauty, his sense of moral goodness, his freedom and the voice of his conscience, with his longings for the infinite and for happiness, man questions himself about God's existence. In all this, he discerns signs of his spiritual soul. The soul, the 'seed of eternity we bear in ourselves, irreducible to the merely material', can have its origin only in God" (33). The reality of our inner life reveals something of God's truth, goodness, and eternity—that God, too, is a personal being and master of all knowledge and goodness.

Yet despite all that nature reveals to us about God, the human person is still not satisfied, nor is God. For to know about something, while interesting, is not the same as to know someone intimately or personally. The human heart longs for love and union with other persons, and that only happens through interpersonal relationships. We desire to share life through mutual self-disclosure and self-giving. In other words, having a merely scientific or philosophical knowledge of another is deeply unsatisfying when what we desire to know is not actually a "what" but a "who." When we say "who," what we mean is the inner self, which is something altogether mysterious and deeply enticing—especially when what we subtly perceive in that mystery is a desire of love directed toward us.

Think about what happens to you when you form an affection for another person. The object of the affection and desire toward that other person is not merely physical. If it were, you would simply look at the other, and that would be the end of it. Yet that is never enough! What draws us to conversation with the other is perhaps a look or glance the other gives you. This glance is really a fleeting glimpse into the soul of that other person. That is what entices you—the eyes of the other invite you to come closer and know him more deeply. The meeting of a desirous glance between two souls is an experience of ecstasy (*ekstasis* in Greek), which refers simply to the "coming out of oneself toward another." We typically think of ecstasy in sexual terms, because sexual intimacy is an especially intense experience of this. A quote from Saint-Exupéry's *Wind, Sand and Stars* captures the point beautifully: "He had the leisure to reflect that it was not those lips he had loved but their pout, not them but the smile. Not those eyes, but their glance. Not the breast, but its gentle swell. He was free to discover at last the source of anguish love had been storing up for him, to learn that it was the unattainable he had been pursuing."[6] Anytime the goodness of another draws us, we experience spiritual ecstasy — or, rather, a drawing out of our spirit to the spirit of another person.

When we think about the other form of God's revelation, what Christians call divine (or special) revelation, we need to keep in mind the reality of intimacy and ecstasy. From the beginning, as humankind searched the stars and wondered in awe, the majesty of creation elicited a desire and a deep inner longing for the One who made all of this. We cannot help ourselves! Have you ever felt deeply moved by the sight of profound beauty — a starry night or a refulgent sunset? When we behold such wonders, it is as though the eternal God, who has no visible face, is looking upon us and drawing us to himself. "Come nearer," he says.

But here is what is even more amazing: God looks upon humankind and all of creation and experiences the same thing — a deep and profound love to be united with all he has made, especially with us. This is why the book of Genesis says, "And God saw everything that he had made, and behold, it was very good [meaning *desirable*]" (1:31). Christians believe that God delights in creation

[6] Antoine de Saint-Exupéry, *Wind, Sand and Stars* (New York: Harcourt, 1992), 196.

and is drawn to it. He desired to do more than just contemplate the goodness of what he had made. He wants to reveal his inner self to us. He wants to experience intimacy with us, and so our inherent goodness draws God out of himself toward us. This is why Genesis also tells us that Adam and Eve "heard the sound of the Lord God walking in the garden" (3:8). God was with them in the Garden of Eden, and their relationship with him was personal. The Church teaches that sin disrupted that friendship, but God never ceased to desire that relationship with the human family. From the beginning, he thus had a plan for restoring that friendship with us. Sacred Scripture reveals that plan to us.

The second book of God's Word (that is, Scripture) is thus the story of how God has consistently pursued this covenant relationship of reconciliation and communion with us, and of how God has opened up his inner self to reveal his purposes and love for the human race. The Bible tells this story. The word *revelation* simply means "unveiling," as in the drawing back of a curtain. The Bible is sacred writing for one main reason, because it unveils to us so much about God's inner self, his longing to be one with us, and his plan to be eternally joined to us through the Incarnation of Jesus Christ. The Bible tells us the deepest truths of our existence, our origins, and end—and the meaning of human life.

The love story of salvation history

Christians believe by faith, then, that Sacred Scripture is the *inspired* Word of God. This means simply that Scripture was not only a revelation about God, but that God was the primary author behind the writing of Scripture. He is the One who is doing the revealing both about himself and about us. Through the Holy Spirit—whom I will introduce later—God inspired the human authors to record this salvific history of God's love for humanity. The Church calls Scripture the Word of God because it reveals God's Eternal Word—that is, the Son of God in and through whom all things were made. We call this story *salvation history*, because God has entered into human history as part of our story, ultimately through the Incarnation of His Word, in order to redeem us from sin.

The image the Bible uses consistently for this relationship is that of marriage. The prophet Ezekiel poetically writes, "I passed by you again and saw that you were now old enough for love. So I spread the corner of my cloak over you to cover your naked-ness; I swore an oath to you and entered into covenant with you … and you became mine" (16:8, NABRE). When Jesus comes, John the Baptist refers to Him as the Bridegroom and to us as the bride (John 3:29). God's plan from the beginning was to enact a spiritual marriage with the human race. Read the Old Testament book Song of Songs for a full rendering of God's covenant love for humanity and our desire for that covenant to be renewed through a Messiah—a Savior.

Since the primary sin God had to root out was the sin of idolatry, Scripture tells mostly about God's gradual redemption of human-kind from false worship and all the sins that come with it. Like a mustard seed, God's plan of salvation began very small; over time, it grew and grew (Mark 4:26–29). Like any loving parent who is trying to discipline a wayward child, God's dealings with humanity had to be an expression of "tough love." Sinfulness made humanity very resistant to God, and so God had to teach us slowly what it means to live a covenant relationship with him. To return to the analogy of marriage, God often used the image of marital infidelity to describe humanity's sinfulness. See the Old Testament book of Hosea as an example.

What the Church calls the *economy of salvation* thus developed in stages. Through each stage, God prepared humanity for the coming of the Bridegroom-Messiah (the Savior), Jesus Christ. The

The Catholic Faith Explained

Father's preparation unfolded through a series of covenants God made with individual people with whom he directly communicated. A covenant is a family bond, like the one created in a marriage. God chose certain people, as his own People, to prepare the way for the coming of Jesus. The Bible is divided into two *testaments* (which means "covenants") — the Old and the New. In the Old Testament books, the Bible tells us that God made five different covenants with different individuals, who all lived within one continuous family lineage or covenant line.

God's covenants with the human family

Here is a brief summary of that covenant line. In later chapters, we will unpack salvation history in more detail. God made the first covenant with Adam and Eve, our first parents. While it remained after their fall from grace, human sin worsened and spread quickly, which is what precipitated the Great Flood. After the Flood, God made the second covenant with the entire human family through Noah, since the entire human race would descend from Noah's line. Again, sin returned very quickly, so the covenant was carried on through the descendants of Noah's son Shem, who remained faithful to God. Eventually, God chose to make a third covenant with Abram (later named Abraham), who was a descendant of Shem.

Through Abraham, God limited his covenant to the tribe of Abraham, but promised the human race that it would be through Abraham's lineage that the Savior would eventually come. God renewed the third covenant within Abraham's lineage through Isaac, Jacob, and then Joseph. Centuries later, under the leadership of Moses, God liberated Abraham's people from slavery in Egypt and established a fourth covenant with the Twelve Tribes (sons) of Jacob. He called them to be a faithful (not idolatrous) nation among the other nations of the ancient world. God called this nation *Israel*. They lived in what today we call the Holy Land, the land God promised to Abraham as part of the covenant. The first five books of Scripture tell the history of salvation up to this point.

The people of Israel grew in strength until they finally became a kingdom under David, with whom God made the fifth covenant. It was a glorious but short-lived time for God's people. Through his covenant with David, God promised that the Messiah would be the son of David (of his lineage). For a complete rendering of this story, you have to read the historical books of the Old Testament — 1 and 2 Samuel, 1 and 2 Kings, and 1 and 2 Chronicles. Idolatry eventually corrupted the kingdom of Israel, and God exiled the Israelites to a foreign land, only to restore their homeland to them after seventy years. During this period of discipline, God led His people through the prophets he sent to teach them His ways.

Throughout the entire period of the Old Covenant, God remained perfectly faithful to his promises, despite the consistent corruption of idolatry and sin. These promises were all fulfilled by the coming of Jesus Christ, the Son of David, who through his death established the sixth covenant, which remains in effect for the entire human race until the end of history. The pivotal figure between the Old and New Testament is John the Baptist. He is the last of the great prophets of Israel and the first disciple of Jesus Christ. John proclaims aloud at the Jordan River, "Behold, the Lamb of God, who takes away the sin of the world! This is he of whom I said, 'After me comes a man who ranks before me, for he was before me.' I myself did not know him; but for this I came baptizing with water, that he might be revealed to Israel" (John 1:29–31).

As the *Catechism* states, quoting the Letter to the Hebrews, "'In many and various ways God spoke of old to our fathers by the prophets, but in these last days he has spoken to us by a

Son.' Christ, the Son of God made man, is the Father's one, perfect and unsurpassable Word. In him he has said everything; there will be no other word than this one" (65). The *Catechism* continues, "'The Christian economy, therefore, since it is the new and definitive Covenant, will never pass away; and no new public revelation is to be expected before the glorious manifestation of our Lord Jesus Christ.' Yet even if Revelation is already complete, it has not been made completely explicit; it remains for Christian faith gradually to grasp its full significance over the course of the centuries" (66).

We believe that God will not reveal any more to us until Jesus returns at the end of history. Jesus is the complete revelation of God's love and purpose for the human race. Throughout the course of Church history, through what the Church calls "private revelation," God has sent his messengers to assist and encourage us. He especially loves to send the Blessed Virgin Mary. For example, research the appearances of Mary at Guadalupe, Mexico; Lourdes, France; and Fatima, Portugal. Yet even so, God has not added any new content to our Faith. Through the Word of God — written into creation and into Scripture — we know all we need to know for salvation and for union with God for all eternity.

Let it suffice that to realize fully our deepest religious aspirations, it is necessary to "read" both books of God's revelation and to draw near to God in love. This is how God opens his heart to us and provides a way to know him personally. Our faith in God and love for him is how we can respond to God's covenant invitation. Just as in any human relationship, when other people make themselves vulnerable by disclosing the deepest affections of their hearts, the appropriate and greatest response we can give is to love them in return. Our relationship with God is no different. As the Church teaches, "Faith is first of all a personal adherence of man to God. At the same time, and inseparably, it is a *free assent to the whole truth that God has revealed.* As personal adherence to God and assent to his truth, Christian faith differs from our faith in any human person. It is right and just to entrust oneself wholly to God and to believe absolutely what he says" (CCC 150).

5

I Am Who I Am

To know that God exists and to desire a personal relationship with him is an important first step toward believing in Him. Yet what is to prevent us from succumbing to the currently popular idea that God is just some impersonal force, as we see in much of the New Age movement? The idea that God is a personal being who cares about us is a long leap. In fact, many life experiences might tell us otherwise, that God is impersonal and just energy or some such thing. In fact, speaking about God from a scientific or philosophical perspective might leave one to think that God is just some faceless being with whom we are unable to have a relationship.

Let us refer back to what we have learned from God's self-revelation. From an outside observer's perspective, knowing God intimately is nearly impossible from our side of the equation. Yet this is the entire point of revelation. According to the Christian Faith, God has shown us his inner life, or to speak more poetically, he has revealed his heart to us. He has revealed his intention and purposes to us in Scripture. He has communicated with us and conveyed that he cares very intimately for human life and for all creatures.

God tells Moses his name

One of the most important stories where we first see God opening up his inner life is when Moses encounters God in the burning bush (Exod. 3:2–6). While Moses is up in the mountains, he happens upon a bush engulfed in fire, but not consumed by the flames. From out of the bush, God speaks to Moses and gives him instructions to liberate his people from bondage in Egypt. God actually declares, "I have seen the affliction of my people who are in Egypt, and have heard their cry because of their taskmasters; I know their sufferings, and I have come down to deliver them out of the hand of the Egyptians, and to bring them up out of that land to a good and broad land, a land flowing with milk and honey" (Exod. 3:7–8).

During this profound encounter that inspires awe in Moses, God expresses his desire to rescue his people from their bondage. The purpose of God's message is that he wants Moses to go on his behalf and rescue the Israelites from their plight. This shows how much God cares about humanity. He does not enjoy seeing us suffer. Rather, he responds to our difficulties and helps us through them. He does this, however, by sending chosen prophets and holy ones to lead us to freedom, especially freedom from sin. During their conversation, God identifies himself as the God of Moses' fathers, of Abraham, Isaac, and Jacob. Not only does God reveal that he has been present to Moses' ancestors, but he also reveals that he is a God of relationship with those who live on the earth, and not merely those who have died. He is God of the living and of life.

In response to the command to go to Egypt and deliver God's people, Moses daringly asks God, "If I come to the people of Israel and say to them, 'The God of your fathers has sent me to you,' and they ask me, 'What is his name?' what shall I say to them?" (Exod. 3:13). In response, God says something of tremendous importance about himself. He tells Moses his name. In Hebrew, the name is *Yahweh*. We translate it simply as "I AM" or "I AM HE WHO IS" or "I AM WHO I AM." All three translations work. At first blush, it sounds like God is being duplicitous by giving Moses a name that is really no name at all. Upon closer reflection, however, we can see the significance of this name through which God reveals his deepest essence, his inner self.

In the ancient world, the name of anything, including the name of a person, always functioned as a description of a creature's nature. We have lost this sense of naming today, because we no longer know the etymology of the names we give to our children; much less do we actually wait long enough to assign a name to a child that suits her personality. We often use nicknames for that. In any case, God actually reveals a lot about himself by this name. Most significantly, it states clearly that he is not another creature or a solitary being alongside other creatures within the cosmos. We are not to interpret God as the biggest being on the block, a god who exists over and against other lesser gods. He is clearly the most powerful being of all, the Almighty, but he does not exist as a being in competition or as a threat to other beings. This is often the problem people have with God—that he is a kind of cosmic bully who threatens us into submission and does violence to our freedom. Yet Scripture says something quite different than that—something quite abstract but terribly profound. God's revelation to Moses tells us that God is *Being* itself.

God is Love

So what is so significant about the fact that God is not *a* being, but *Being* itself? From the Christian perspective, it means that God is distinct from creation, and not a part of it, so we are not to confuse him for something finite and corruptible. This is important, because it means that no imperfection of any kind can be part of God—there is no mixture of good and evil in him. There is only perfection, for he is the fullness of *being* in himself. This is critical, because no condition of existence can limit God. God has no need for anything. Thus, whatever he creates and does is a gift given for our sakes and not for any need of his own—because he has no need. He is the plenitude of every perfection, and all things he has made participate in what he himself is. God does not need anything from us. Everything he commands is for our good, not his.

If we ponder the fact that God is the fullness of *being* and that he has no need of anything, we then have to ask ourselves an important question: *why*, then, would God create everything in the first place? The question of "why" is an indispensable question. If he has no need for creatures, then there must be another reason, so what is it? With some more reflection, we can discern that God created us because he wanted to—it was his good pleasure to create us. He created us because he wanted to share with us a portion of his own being and goodness as a gift. He wanted every creature—and humans especially—to participate in existence and life. We can find no other reason God would create everything otherwise. A being who is *being* itself can create other beings only out of love. This is why Genesis tells us, "God saw everything that he had made, and behold, it was very good" (1:31).

In philosophy, we have an important principle that will help us understand this better. The principle is that *being* and *goodness* are convertible terms. What this means is that "to be" is to be "good." Things that exist are desirable and of great value and dignity. This is true of all things that exist—all things have some measure of goodness and value. When we speak about evil, we are actually speaking about the absence of some reality that ought to be there. For example, we call blindness a physical *evil*, because the eyes lack the vision they ought to have. What is absent is the good of sight.

In moral matters, we say that murder is evil, because a murderous act lacks the love for human life that ought to be there. For God to say to Moses "I AM" is thus to say "I am *goodness* itself" too. In him is no evil, for nothing is lacking in God. This is why he cares for the plight of his people in slavery.

To elaborate further, God is not the universe, but something entirely distinct from it, which is why he is able to love it perfectly without any self-interest, but as pure gift. St. John says this concisely: "He who does not love does not know God; for God is love " (1 John 4:8). He can say this truthfully, because God is the One from whom all goodness flows. This is most obvious in the gift of God's Son, Jesus, who died for our sins. Thus, St. John goes on to say, " In this the love of God was made manifest among us, that God sent his only Son into the world, so that we might live through him. In this is love, not that we loved God but that he loved us and sent his Son to be the expiation for our sins" (1 John 4:9–10). St Paul says something similar: "God shows his love for us in that while we were yet sinners Christ died for us" (Rom. 5:8). Therefore, when God speaks to Moses in the burning bush, he says to him in effect, "I am the One in whom all created beings find their origin and existence. All things originate in me and are good. I love them — each and every one. I am the One who is full of mercy and love for my people."

But let us push this concept of *being* even further. St. Paul once professed to an audience in Athens the following:

> The God who made the world and everything in it, being the
> Lord of heaven and earth, does not live in shrines made by
> man, nor is he served by human hands ... since he himself
> gives to all men life and breath and everything. And he made
> from one every nation of men on all the face of the earth
> ... that they should seek God, in the hope that they might

feel after him and find him. Yet he is not far from each of us, for "In him we live and move and have our being" ... "for indeed we are his offspring." (Acts 17:24–26, 27–28)

To say that in God "we live, and move, and have our being" and that we are his offspring is to say that we *share* in God's own being, such that any goodness we perceive in ourselves, we can attribute to God in perfect measure. For example, one might say of herself, "I am merciful." Of God, we would say he is *mercy* itself. Of an attractive woman, we might say she is beautiful. Of God, we would say that he is *beauty* itself. The woman is beautiful because she bears in herself the image of beauty that belongs to God alone. He is perfect, full of *being* in every respect and lacking nothing. We can say the same of any perfection we find in ourselves — strength, patience, generosity, kindness, humility, and so forth. God is the perfection of every creature, and all created perfections are but a reflection of God's perfection.

Scripture tells us that God made us in his image and likeness. We bear a very special resemblance to the Creator that other earthly creatures do not share (CCC 33). We have intellect and will. Therefore, we are able to know what is true, and we can will what is good and act with freedom for the sake of love. We are persons and not mere things. By reflecting on this for a moment, we can thus come to see that God must be *truth* and *goodness* itself and perfect *freedom* all in one. This makes God a personal presence, not an impersonal force. That is, God is conscious and free to act in a manner that far exceeds our greatest feats of knowledge and freedom. How could an impersonal force create personal beings? The challenge, however, is to believe that God has a personal interest in your existence and in your life. It is through revelation, like the revelation given to Moses, that we learn how deeply God cares for every person and desires to be in relationship with us.

I Am Who I Am

The revelation of God to Moses is one of the most important moments Scripture records. It shows us that God is an integral player in human life—even if we are not personally aware of this. Christians do not believe that God is merely aware of our lives, but that he has done amazing things for us. St. Paul professes beautifully how deeply God cares for human life: "But God, who is rich in mercy, out of the great love with which he loved us, even when we were dead through our trespasses, made us alive together with Christ (by grace you have been saved), and raised us up with him, and made us sit with him in the heavenly places in Christ Jesus, that in the coming ages he might show the immeasurable riches of his grace in kindness toward us in Christ Jesus" (Eph. 2:4–7). This declaration of faith in the God of Jesus Christ sums up perfectly who God is for Christians. Through Jesus Christ, we have a clear knowledge that God is rich in mercy, perfect in love, and the fullness of all that is good. In the following chapters, we will learn more about what God has revealed to us about himself and his intentions toward humanity.

6

The Difference Faith Makes

As we have seen thus far, faith and reason are not opposed to each other but help us attain truth in different ways. Faith is an important pathway to truth because it allows us to accept God's self-revelation. Through faith, we can know God more intimately and understand his will for our lives. Even more importantly, we can trust his Word, believe in it, and live our lives by it. This is what faith is all about! Faith is our response to God's revelation. Throughout the rest of this book, we will look in detail at what, specifically, God has revealed to us. In the meantime, let it suffice to say that what we comprehend of God's Word resonates very intensely within our hearts and affirms our deepest longings and aspirations for things such as friendship, love, justice, mercy, communion, and a whole host of other very human longings. When we encounter God in a personal way, it is natural for us to respond to him by seeking a relationship with him in faith — by believing in him. Any human relationship is the same way.

God has a plan for us

The importance of Christian faith becomes more evident, however, once we understand all that God has actually revealed and why Christians call this *good news*. Throughout salvation history, God has revealed to us his plan of loving goodness. The first paragraph of the *Catechism* states the following:

> God, infinitely perfect and blessed in himself, in a plan of sheer goodness *freely created man to make him share in his own blessed life*. For this reason, at every time and in every place, *God draws close to man*. He calls man to seek him, to know him, to love him with all his strength. He calls together all men, scattered and divided by sin, into the unity of his family, the Church. To accomplish this, when the fullness of time had come, God sent his Son as Redeemer and Savior. In his Son and through him, *he invites men to become, in the Holy Spirit, his adopted children* and thus heirs of his blessed life. (Emphasis mine)

This is God's whole plan in one paragraph. This is the story that Scripture tells: namely, that God desired to make his plan of loving goodness known to us, so that by faith, we might respond in love and enter into God's family, which is called the Church. Only in the response of faith do our lives fully connect with God's great purpose for us. Reason alone cannot quite make that connection to God's plan. We know from historical evidence that aside from God's covenant people, the human race was entirely ignorant of this plan. It simply does not show up in any ancient writings other than the Bible. In this chapter, I would like simply to provide a basic sketch of the Christian Faith as Catholics believe God has revealed it. We call this basic proclamation the *kerygma*. In the remaining chapters, I will unpack the *kerygma* in more detail.

The good news of Jesus Christ

The Church sums up the entire plan of God in one name — Jesus Christ. Jesus teaches us to have faith in the true God who created us. As the Eternal Son of God, he alone expresses the entire revelation of God's plan. Through him, we enter into communion with God, in order to know God in a personal and intimate way and, even more, to share fully in the mystery of God's being. Faith in Jesus Christ thus helps us discover who we are, why we are here, and for what purpose God desires us to live our lives to the fullest. The faith we have in Jesus makes us children of God. He shows us that our ultimate purpose is to live eternally as part of God's covenant family. To have this faith makes us Jesus' disciples, followers of what the early Christians called *the Way*.

Scripture clearly teaches us that the only way to the Father is by having faith in Jesus: "Jesus said ... 'I am the way, and the truth, and the life; no one comes to the Father, but by me'" (John 14:6). This is why Christians call Jesus *Lord*. Jesus shows us that the way to the Father is that of humility, service, and personal sacrifice. This is why St. Paul professes, "Though he was in the form of God, [Jesus] did not regard equality with God something to be grasped. Rather, he emptied himself, taking the form of a slave ... God greatly exalted him and bestowed on him the name that is above every name, that at the name of Jesus every knee should bend, of those in heaven and on earth and under the earth, and every tongue confess that Jesus Christ is Lord, to the glory of God the Father" (Phil. 2:6–7, 9–11, NABRE). Jesus thus reveals the deepest meaning of human existence, and he reveals that the only path to eternal life is divine love: "For God so loved the world that he gave his only Son, that whoever believes in him should not perish but have eternal life" (John 3:16).

By faith, when we accept Jesus as Lord and receive the power of the Holy Spirit through baptism, God gives us the ability to live differently than we could otherwise on our own. In an age so enamored by superheroes, our society forgets what it once professed: that Christian discipleship is a path to supernatural life.

The Catholic Faith Explained

Here is what St. Peter says in one of his letters: "His divine power has bestowed on us everything that makes for life and devotion, through the knowledge of him who called us by his own glory and power. Through these, he has bestowed on us the precious and very great promises, so that through them *you may come to share in the divine nature*, after escaping from the corruption that is in the world because of evil desire" (2 Pet. 1:3–4, NABRE, emphasis mine).

Faith is not a blind leap, therefore, but rather a person's complete surrender to the truth that God is love and has made us *for* love in his Son Jesus Christ (1 John 4:8). The *Catechism* states, "God's very being is love. By sending his only Son and the Spirit of Love in the fullness of time, God has revealed his innermost secret: God himself is an eternal exchange of love, Father, Son, and Holy Spirit, and he has destined us to share in that exchange" (221). Elsewhere, the *Catechism* states, "God, who 'dwells in unapproachable light', wants to communicate his own divine life to the men he freely created, in order to adopt them as his sons in his only-begotten Son. By revealing himself God wishes to make them capable of responding to him, and of knowing him and of loving him far beyond their own natural capacity" (52).

Why the Christian religion is liberating

Today some people scoff at the Christian religion—and religion in general. The word *religion* seems to get a bad rap, implying that religion enslaves us to an ideology and infringes on our freedom. Some people even go so far as to say that religious people are unenlightened and prescientific, meaning we do not think for ourselves and live our lives full of ignorance and superstition. More and more, religious people are called "haters" and are caricatured as bigots. Karl Marx stated that "religion is the opiate of the people," meaning that religious faith is like a drug that simply pacifies a difficult life or a troubled soul. The implication is that there is no basis in reality for religion. Faith is just a private fiction. You might also hear some people say, "I am a spiritual person but I do not do organized religion."

The Enlightenment gave us these views of religion. The Enlightenment was an eighteenth-century philosophical movement that denied the value of Christian faith and maintained that reason alone could lead us to truth and solve the problem of evil. All we had to do was figure out ways to improve human life through science, and all would be well. The architects of this new way of thinking also believed that God was distant and disengaged from our lives, like a clockmaker who just wound up the world and let it tick away. Some denied God's existence altogether. The Enlightenment occurred well over two hundred years ago, and society has advanced immensely in the arena of science and technology, but have we seen a significant improvement in the quality of human existence? Are people happier for having believed less in God and more in reason and technology? Does your smartphone settle your soul and bring joy to your inner self? Do modern travel and social media make you feel closer and more connected to others, or constantly unsure of yourself and fragmented? Do the comforts of convenience bring peace to the soul? It seems not.

What is religion, anyhow? The word *religion* comes from the word *ligare*, which means "to bind." By religious observance, human beings will bind themselves to *something* as a matter of conviction and personal devotion. For example, a person who has a goal of going to the Olympics will bind himself "religiously" to the practice and devotion of the training required to attend the games. As it turns out, every person binds himself or herself to some "religious" observance. Today, it might be yoga, veganism, or some other fitness lifestyle, or a new age practice like Wicca. For others, it might be politics or their professional occupation. Human beings have an innate need to bind their lives to a purpose. Otherwise, we go a little crazy in the head. Human beings cannot be idle, or we lose our sanity.

The Church would suggest that history took a wrong turn a while back by trying to convince us that we did not need traditional religion or faith in God, that we could find purpose in material things and the endless consumption of whatever satisfactions the marketplace could produce. Those who taught such things seem to have been profoundly mistaken. It is not that material things are evil, but they do not satisfy the soul. While material advances are good, when we convince ourselves that we no longer need God or religion and then attempt to fulfill our deepest longings through material things, we end up miserable. In fact, we tend to war within ourselves and with each other and tear one another apart as we implode psychologically. That is why so many people today are lost in substance abuse, sexual escapism, violent activism, and perpetual distraction. Too many people today are depressed and even questioning if their existence has any meaning. If people feel this way, it is not because our lives *are* meaningless, but because the world is trying to convince us that the meaning of our lives is to satisfy the urges of the body, rather than the longings of the soul for true love.

Whom shall I serve?

The Christian religion thus always boils down to a decision. To what am I going to bind myself? What is going to most fulfill my deepest longings? Is it yoga? Is it making money or having sex? Is it athletic competition? Is it protesting or changing my gender? What is it? In the end, all of our "religious" observances, whether we believe this or not, are a personal quest for the true religion. While we modern people like to convince ourselves that we invent religion for ourselves, we seem always to come up short. Thus, perhaps the better question is not what I will bind myself to, but whom. Maybe materialism does not satisfy, because the satisfaction of my body is not the purpose of my life. Perhaps the satisfaction of my soul is the purpose. However, what the soul most desires is true love, and that requires an absolute and complete union with God, who *is* love.

While we might be tempted at this point to conclude that human relationships will bring us ultimate and perfect satisfaction, the Christian Faith professes that only God is capable of satisfying an infinite desire for love, which is what we have. In other words, our innate tendency toward religious observance is meant for God, who is the only One to whom we can bind ourselves and thus fulfill our deepest longings for meaning. God is the only One who cannot be an idol for us. To place our happiness in anything else other than God is to become idle and thus to lose our happiness. My play on words here is intentional. Idolatry is really idleness. We become idle (restless) when we place our ultimate happiness in anything other than God. St. Augustine has a famous quote about this that Christians often cite: "You have made us for yourself, and our hearts are restless until they rest in you" (quoted in CCC 30). This is the essential meaning and purpose of worship. Worship is ultimately about having a right and disciplined relationship with God, in the manner God has revealed as the best way to find happiness in him. True worship brings peace to the human heart.

Is there such a thing as true religion?

What, then, does Christian faith result in? *True religion.* By placing our faith in the God who has revealed himself to us in Jesus Christ, we can at last fully bind ourselves to God, who will satisfy our deepest longing for love. Christians call their religion the *true* religion, not because Christian disciples are superior to people of other faiths, but because Christians believe that faith in Jesus leads directly to union with God. In Jesus, God loves us perfectly, and he will receive all our love in return. This is why Jesus ordains the Faith to the communion of the faithful, which we call the *Church*. Jesus established the Church as his Body before he ascended into Heaven to be with the Father. As St. Paul states, "For just as the body is one and has many members, and all the members of the body, though many, are one body, so it is with Christ. For by one Spirit we were all baptized into one body—Jews or Greeks, slaves or free—and all were made to drink of one Spirit" (1 Cor. 12:12–13).

Christians, therefore, believe that the fullest reality of religion is not private but resides in the communion of the Church. Christian faith is not individualistic, but communal. A disciple does not believe alone, for there is no such thing as a solitary Christian. *We* believe! The entire Church professes faith in the revelation of Jesus Christ. As such, Christians also believe that the Church is necessary for salvation. Through the Church alone, we encounter Jesus, come to faith in him, and receive the Holy Spirit, so that together we may reach the Father in Heaven. This explains why, as a matter of faith, Christians also believe *in* the Church. I will explain these last points further toward the end of this book.

Any Christian must confess that over the centuries, the Church has experienced divisions because of the sinfulness of her members. These divisions have been very harmful to the faithful and to the credibility of the Christian religion—and have even been a terrible scandal at times! Christians have warred against others and even against each other, which has caused some people to reject the truth of the Christian Faith and even religion altogether. This explains why St. Paul urges us, "Preserve the unity of the spirit through the bond of peace: one body and one Spirit, as you were also called to the one hope of your call; one Lord, one faith, one baptism; one

God and Father of all, who is over all and through all and in all" (Eph. 4:3–6, NABRE). St. Paul is encouraging Christians to fulfill Jesus' prayer for the Church: "I pray not only for them, but also for those who will believe in me through their word, so that they may all be one, as you, Father, are in me and I in you, that they also may be in us, *that the world may believe that you sent me*" (John 17:20–21, NABRE emphasis mine).

To conclude this chapter, faith in the God of Jesus Christ is not a blind leap into foolishness. It is the simple act of taking God's hand trustingly into our own and walking toward the Light of Life. Faith is our humble response to the God who has revealed his infinite love to us through the revelation of his Son, Jesus Christ, the Eternal Word of God. Faith is how we reach God in Heaven. As Jesus himself says, "I am the light of the world. Whoever follows me will not walk in darkness, but will have the light of life" (John 8:12). Faith is a light on the path of life. It secures for us the essential truths we need if we are to lead lives full of joy and happiness. Without faith, Christians believe, the human family remains in darkness, blinded by sin, and the human longing for love remains unsatisfied. This is a bold claim, I know, but one made not in arrogance, but in the humble awareness of our own personal sinfulness.

7

Revelation and Religious Pluralism

As we saw in the last chapter, some individuals might mock people of faith, because such individuals are of the opinion that faith prevents us from thinking for ourselves. Certain scientists disparage the idea of faith as an outdated superstition. In a scientific age, the belief is that only science gives us an accurate picture of reality. Thus, the idea of *atheism* has become more popular recently. Atheism is the belief that God does not exist. Some atheists have a purely materialistic view of the world and deny the spiritual dimension of reality. Another growing perspective is *agnosticism*, which describes people who refuse to commit to any particular religion or idea of God. Agnostics remain open to any religious possibility without committing to one in particular. From a Christian perspective, these ways of dealing with the question of God say more about people's desire to be free in matters of faith than they do about any philosophical arguments people have made about God himself.

Yet if religious faith is so unreasonable, then why do so many people practice it? Let us consider the fact that, throughout the Western world (as of 2018), roughly 75 percent of people say they believe in God, while less than 5 percent actually say they are atheists. An even higher percentage of people in Africa and Latin

America believe in God. It remains a persistent fact that the vast majority of people throughout the ages have believed in God or in some "higher power." The pervasive belief in God suggests quite powerfully that faith is quite reasonable. What can cause concern for the more reflective person is why humankind has so many different ideas about God and religion. The diversity of belief can lead one to think that faith in the existence of God is not "objective" truth, but a matter of subjective opinion.

Why so many religions?

That most people believe in God, but hold different ideas about him, is something one can explain without too much difficulty, however. The fact that so many people believe in God, and *have* believed in him since the beginning of human history, suggests that belief in God is the most reasonable point of view. To deny this would be like asserting that love does not exist, despite the fact that everyone believes in it. To assume that rational beings would so consistently believe in the existence of something that did not exist is itself irrational. Yet religious pluralism is a fact as well. The presence of different religions in the world simply suggests that various cultures relate to God differently.

Religious diversity is an expression of human cultures, which differ from one another. This is why Christianity believes that divine revelation is so important. Revelation helps us distinguish between true and false notions of God, and yet by revealing himself, God intends no harm to the distinctiveness of various human cultures. He welcomes different religious expressions, so long as we maintain an adherence to the truths about him and his purpose for us. This, however, has been the biggest challenge for humankind. Over the centuries, at least from a Christian perspective, many ideas about God have arisen that, upon close examination, seem unreasonable. These portrayals of who God is and what God wills for us seem discordant with God's nature and human flourishing.

One criterion for determining whether particular notions of God are correct is philosophical reasoning itself. Not only can we know that God exists, but we can also use reason to demonstrate certain attributes of God, thus eliminating false conceptions of him. As the Church puts it, "In defending the ability of human reason to know God, the Church is expressing her confidence in the possibility of speaking about him to all men and with all men, and therefore of dialogue with other religions, with philosophy and science, as well as with unbelievers and atheists" (CCC 39). Once we establish that God exists, we can reason to a knowledge of God's most essential attributes. Yet, and this is critical, "God transcends all creatures. We must therefore continually purify our language of everything in it that is limited, image-bound or imperfect, if we are not to confuse our image of God — 'the inexpressible, the incomprehensible, the invisible, the ungraspable' — with our human representations. Our human words always fall short of the mystery of God" (CCC 42).

For example, reason can discover that God is *one*; that he is pure *spirit*; that he is *all-powerful*; that he is *all-knowing*; and that he is perfectly *simple* in his existence, and thus not a composite being made of many parts, like we are. Reason can show that he is *eternal* and beyond time. St. Thomas Aquinas offers a wonderful example of how philosophical thought can discern certain attributes of God in the first part of his famous work, the *Summa Theologiae*, questions 1–26. All of these things philosophy can demonstrate, once the mind grasps that God exists. Hence, "In speaking about God like this, our language is using human modes of expression; nevertheless it really does attain to God himself, though unable to express him in his infinite simplicity" (CCC 43). The important point is that we maintain a clear distinction between the mystery of God, who is *ineffable* (beyond our expressions), and our notions of God, which can attain to some truths about God.

The problem of idolatry

Unfortunately, because of intellectual error and because of sin, which we will consider in later chapters, one of the consequences of fallen human nature is that we easily fall into superstition. We invent false notions of God, or, even worse, worship things that are not God at all, but only creatures God made, such as the sun and the earth. We can also commit horrible offenses against one another in the name of God and faith. Such crimes, however, have no place in Christianity or any sincere religious expression. Not only do they offend God, but they also offend human reason. The book of Wisdom describes well the folly of false notions of God:

> Foolish by nature were all who were in ignorance of God, and who from the good things seen did not succeed in knowing the one who is, and from studying the works did not discern the artisan; Instead either fire, or wind, or the swift air, or the circuit of the stars, or the mighty water, or the luminaries of heaven, the governors of the world, they considered gods. Now if out of joy in their beauty they thought them gods, let them know how far more excellent is the Lord than these; for the original source of beauty fashioned them. Or if they were struck by their might and energy, let them realize from these things how much more powerful is the one who made them. For from the greatness and the beauty of created things their original author, by analogy, is seen ... For they have gone astray perhaps,

though they seek God and wish to find him. For they search busily among his works, but are distracted by what they see, because the things seen are fair ... For if they so far succeeded in knowledge that they could speculate about the world, how did they not more quickly find its Lord? (13:1–5, 6–7, 9, NABRE)

Early on in human history, disparate cultures developed different notions of God based upon their fascination with the created order, instead of what creation might have taught them about the Creator. Let us look at some of these mistaken notions.

We call the belief that God and creation are the same thing *pantheism*. Many of the more primitive religions of the world were (and still are) pantheistic, meaning that they do not philosophically grasp that God is not the same thing as creation but is distinct from creation and infinitely greater than the created order. Today, we see the belief in Gaia, which is a pantheistic religion of earth worship. Another common misunderstanding of the ancient world is *polytheism*. This also is rooted in a pantheistic view of creation, but it differs in that some peoples believed in many gods instead of just one God. While polytheistic peoples might have believed that one of these gods was the greatest, they did not believe in *monotheism*—that there is only one God and he is completely distinct from his creation. Each of these different beliefs was surrounded by a tradition of mythology, which in narrative form attempted to explain the origins of the world and the pantheon of the gods. Think for example of ancient Greek mythology.

In the ancient Middle East and Asia, not long before the time of Christ, some cultures went through a period of philosophical enlightenment, whereby philosophy began to purify mythological notions of God. This happened in ancient Greece and China, for example. These philosophical movements all converged on the idea of monotheism—that philosophically, God has to be one. This is what reason tells us. These philosophers came to this conclusion without any exposure to Sacred Scripture, at least as far as we know. This was around the same time, however, that the people of Israel also came definitely through revelation to faith in the one God and to the belief that there was no other God but him alone. What differentiated the Israelites from all the other nations was that their relationship with God was intimate and personal—or as Christians would say, *covenantal*.

Thus, around the same time, both faith and reason came to the same truth that God is one and there is no other. As an aside, when Europeans discovered Native American peoples in the sixteenth century, some of those cultures were monotheistic, professing belief in a Father Spirit. They also believed in *animism*, which is the idea that other creatures were deities (gods), but they strikingly believed that there was one Supreme Being—a universal Father. This shows two things. First, some cultures seem to have preserved the prehistorical memory of the One God better than others did. Second, not all ancient peoples had fallen completely into idolatry—the worship of false gods.

We call these traces of the true religion and worship of God *preambles of faith*. Every culture has certain traces or seeds of the original truths about God known from natural reason or primordial memory, which truths they handed down by oral tradition and storytelling. This is one of the reasons so many ancient peoples converted to Christianity when they heard the gospel. These preambles of true religion had existed among these peoples for centuries, and so they were well disposed to accept the Judeo-Christian revelation of God, which helped these peoples come to a more complete understanding of the God they had worshiped, perhaps indefinably. The Church teaches that the most fundamental reason these preambles of faith existed is that God has written on the human heart a desire for him, and we can intuitively know that the One God exists. The reason for the development of false notions of God, as we will see in a later chapter, is that human error and sinfulness perverted our notions of God for the sake of power and sexual exploitation.

The Judeo-Christian God and the religions of the world

What emerged out of the ancient world because of divine revelation were three monotheistic religions, all of which professed belief in the God of Israel, although each had different ideas about him. These three religions are Judaism, Christianity, and Islam. The Jewish faith professes to this day its faith in Yahweh—the God of Abraham. The *Catechism* states, "The Jewish faith, unlike other non-Christian religions, is already a response to God's revelation in the Old Covenant. To the Jews 'belong the sonship, the glory, the covenants, the giving of the law, the worship, and the promises; to them belong the patriarchs, and of their race, according to the flesh, is the Christ', 'for the gifts and the call of God are irrevocable'" (839). Christians also believe in Yahweh, but believe that Jesus Christ revealed further that Yahweh—the One God—exists as the Holy Trinity—Father, Son, and Holy Spirit. I will look at that belief in the next chapter.

Centuries later, the Prophet Muhammad established a new religion in the Middle East that represented a return to the Old Testament God of Abraham, but under the name of *Allah*. Muslims "profess to hold the faith of Abraham, and together with us they adore the one, merciful God, mankind's judge on the last day" (CCC 841). The Church acknowledges that all three religions profess belief in the one God of Abraham, but teaches that Jesus' teaching about God represents the fullest and most accurate revelation of who God is in himself.

The Catholic Faith Explained

When we look at all the other religious traditions around the world, we see belief in the existence of God, but a diversity of ideas about him. The Hindu religion, for example, has brought an ancient form of polytheism and animism into the modern world. As to all other religious traditions, the Church "recognizes in other religions that search, among shadows and images, for the God who is unknown yet near since he gives life and breath and all things and wants all men to be saved. Thus, the Church considers all goodness and truth found in these religions as 'a preparation for the Gospel and given by him who enlightens all men that they may at length have life'" (CCC 843).

Other so-called religions, such as Buddhism and Confucianism, are not, properly speaking, religions, but philosophies of life based upon the teachings of a philosophical master. People adhere to them "religiously" as a form of discipline, but these philosophies lack the relational dimension of true religion. They tend to focus on ways to live one's life with greater intentionality and mindfulness (that is, ethically), but do not necessarily espouse the worship of God or religious practice. That is not to say that the founders of these philosophical movements did not believe in God or have a religion; it is just that their philosophy is not about God, but about the nature of human existence. It is more helpful to compare Buddhism to the Academy of Plato than to Judaism or Islam, much less Christianity.

Also important to mention is the philosophical notion of God known as *Deism*. This is the God of the philosophers during Europe's eighteenth-century Enlightenment. They believed in God's existence and that he was responsible for all of creation, including the dignity and freedom of humanity. However, they also held to a mechanistic view of creation and thus believed that God was not personally involved in the world. He existed, rather, at a distance and simply upheld the laws of nature. This remains a very common view of God today, which the Church calls a form of practical atheism. This means living as though God does not care what we do or as though God is not involved with our lives.

These other philosophies are not incompatible necessarily with the convictions of the Christian Faith. This is true especially when it comes to certain ethical ideas, which find their origins in natural reason and law. As Pope St. John Paul II famously stated in *Fides et ratio*:

> Philosophy's powerful influence on the formation and de-velopment of the cultures of the West should not obscure the influence it has also had upon the ways of understanding existence found in the East. Every people has its own na-tive and seminal wisdom which, as a true cultural treasure, tends to find voice and develop in forms which are genu-inely philosophical ... Driven by the desire to discover the ultimate truth of existence, human beings seek to acquire those universal elements of knowledge which enable them to understand themselves better and to advance in their own self-realization. These fundamental elements of knowledge spring from the *wonder* awakened in them by the contempla-tion of creation. (Nos. 3, 4)

Nevertheless, from a Christian perspective, these philosophies provide a limited view of God in need of the more complete view that divine revelation provides.

The Church respects humankind's religious nature and affirms it over and against atheism or agnosticism. It is more honest to strive sincerely after true religion, even if mistaken, than to reject religion altogether as contrary to reason. As the *Catechism* states, "Atheism is often based on a false conception of human autonomy, exaggerated to the point of refusing any dependence on God" (2126). Nevertheless, the Church also believes strongly in religious liberty and that all people must freely seek the truth about God and never be forced to believe in God. The Church thus strikes a healthy balance between the human obligation to religious truth and the human right to religious freedom:

> "All men are bound to seek the truth, especially in what concerns God and his Church, and to embrace it and hold on to it as they come to know it." This duty derives from "the very dignity of the human person." It does not contradict a "sincere respect" for different religions which frequently "reflect a ray of that truth which enlightens all men," nor the requirement of charity, which urges Christians "to treat with love, prudence and patience those who are in error or ignorance with regard to the faith." (CCC 2104)

That God exists is an essential truth of human experience and is necessary for living a fully human life. While we can observe different religious traditions down through the centuries, we must affirm the religious nature of humankind and respect the freedom of every person and every people to express that relationship to God, as they are able.

8

The God of Jesus Christ

To this point, we have considered that God exists and that he is an almighty being, who is one, eternal, and distinct from the universe, and so forth. We also saw that God is a loving being who wills good for his creatures. The biblical idea that creation is "very good" helps us see further that the only reason God would have created everything in the first place is that he is the perfection of love. However, the idea that God created out of love helps us understand only God's relationship to us. He wanted to share his life and goodness with beings other than himself, especially other persons. Yet the biblical idea that "God is love" goes much deeper, penetrating into the mystery of who God is. Probably the greatest value of divine revelation is that it opens up a window into God's inner life and helps us understand better who God is within himself.

Belief in the Holy Trinity, that God is one in three Persons, is the central truth of the Christian Faith. This revelation of God about himself is what most distinguishes the Christian religion from every other religion in the history of the human race. In fact, this revelation about God is what ultimately explains how it is that God is love. Let us look more closely at what Jesus reveals about the Trinity and how this belief shapes the core of what we profess in the Creed. As mysterious as it sounds, "God is one but not solitary" (CCC 254). In this chapter, we need to grasp what it means to say that God is Father, Son, and Holy Spirit—that he is one God in three Persons.

In theology, we make a distinction between the *economic* Trinity and the *immanent* Trinity. When we speak about the economic Trinity, we are referring to what God does in creation, his mighty works, and the feats he accomplishes in human history. When we speak about the immanent Trinity, we are referring to God's inner self. In a similar way, human beings also have an immanent and an economic self. We perform outward works for others to see, but we also have a private inner life that no one sees or knows unless we share it with him. Other people's knowledge of you only grows as people pay attention to your words about yourself and your actions. The same is true of God; we can know some things about God's inner life by what he says about himself and by what he does. In fact, through the stories recorded in Sacred Scripture, he has shared a lot about his inner life. We call this historical expression of God's words and deeds the *economy of salvation*—hence, the term economic Trinity. The Church uses the word *economy* in this way to describe how God manages his *oikos*, which means "household" in Greek. By how God governs and provides for creation (God's house) and redeems humanity from sin, we learn much about who God is in himself.

The Bible tells us that God has saved us from sin through the redemptive works of three Eternal Persons—the Father, the Son, and the Holy Spirit. Yet the Bible does not exactly explain what this means or how this can be. How can God be one but, at the same time, three Persons? Does this mean that there are three gods? Does it mean that God relates to us in three distinct ways? Does it mean that God has different modes of existence according to which we are to call Him by three different names? The early Church did not know exactly how to answer these questions. What the Church did know was that she was to baptize in the name of the Father, the Son, and the Holy Spirit (Matt. 28:19). We also know that Jesus addressed the Father and the Spirit in a personal way, while also referring to himself as God (Matt. 11:27; John 10:30; 14:15–17).

In the First Letter of John, we read, "No one who denies the Son has the Father. He who confesses the Son has the Father also" (2:23). In the Gospel of John, Jesus describes the inner life of God and our participation in that life like this: "Father ... I wish that where I am they [the disciples] also may be with me, that they may see my glory that you gave me, because you loved me before the foundation of the world. Righteous Father, the world also does not know you, but I know you, and they know that you sent me. I made known to them your name and I will make it known, that the love [the Spirit] with which you loved me may be in them and I in them" (17:24–25, NABRE).

The Church spent over three centuries figuring out how to understand and explain this central mystery of the Christian Faith. It was unique and unprecedented to think of God as a trinity, especially the God of Israel, who stated repeatedly that he is one God (see Deut. 6:4 for a well-known example). With the help of certain philosophical concepts, the Church eventually defined the doctrine of the Trinity and was able to explain how God can exist as three-in-one. The Church did not invent the teaching on the Trinity, but had to clarify what exactly Christianity believed about who Jesus revealed God to be. Down through the centuries, many great teachers of the Faith have used various analogies from creation to explain the Trinity. You have probably heard the three-leaf clover analogy that St. Patrick used—a clover is one flower with three petals. This is helpful for a little child, but let us look at a couple of other analogies that actually make the doctrine of the Trinity come into clearer focus.

The Catholic Faith Explained

The trinitarian nature of God

The first analogy is that of the sun. If you think about it, the sun is one, but the word *sun* refers to three things, all of which make the sun what it is. In fact, without one of these, the sun would not be a star. The first and not-so-obvious feature of the sun is that it is pure nuclear fusion. Only recently have scientists discovered this. The second feature is that the sun is light. A burning mass of energy emits light that travels to earth in the form of sunshine. Finally, the sun is heat. The light that travels from the burning ball of gas generates heat. The heat we feel is also the sun. The sun is one thing, but exists in three ways—as a ball of nuclear fusion, as emitted light, and as heat that proceeds from a generative fire and its light. Each is distinct, but together they are one thing. While no analogy is perfect, the sun helps us see how God can be a Father who generates the Son, and how together they generate the Spirit, while remaining one thing.

A second analogy is a river, which is one, but also means three distinct things. A river originates from a source, a point of origin from which the water flows. This could be a spring or a multitude of creeks that finally converge to become a river. The headwaters of the river are where it originates. The second aspect of a river is the course by which the river flows. A river is comprised of riverbanks. Finally, the water that flows from the source through the banks is the river also. Without a source, the banks, and the water, we do not have a river. Each is distinct from the other, yet together they form one thing, a river. The analogy of a river helps us comprehend how God the Father is a source for both the Son and the Spirit.

Two more analogies for understanding the Trinity, and probably the most important ones, come from our knowledge of the human person. St. Augustine gave us the first, which we call the *psychological* model of the Trinity. St. Augustine realized that within the soul of a human person, which God made in his own image, we find three things that comprise the inner self. The first is the human spirit, which is the source of both the mind and the will. From the mind proceeds an inner word of self-knowledge. St. Augustine explains that this is analogous to the Eternal Son, who proceeds from the Father as an Eternal Word. From the human spirit, we also find a movement of will that proceeds as a love for self. Thus, the self is comprised of three things in one — a spirit, from which there is a procession of self-knowledge and self-love — a kind of image of the Trinity. This analogy is more abstract, but it is not impossible to understand how, within each person's inner life, we discover a trinity of spirit and the processions of self-knowledge and self-love.

Within the last century, Pope St. John Paul II taught us what we call the *personalist* model of the Trinity, which is the final analogy we will consider. We have already looked briefly at this one. God reveals his inner life through the communion of love that exists between human beings, especially a husband, wife, and their children within a family. By coming together in a conjugal union of mutual self-gift, a husband and wife give rise to a child, which is the fruit of their loving communion. This analogy helps us understand how, through the unity between the Father and the Son, a procession of love occurs, which is the Person of the Holy Spirit. The Holy Spirit is *the spirit of love* between the Father and the Son.

The *Catechism* says, "The Christian family is a communion of persons, a sign and image of the communion of the Father and the Son in the Holy Spirit" (2205). What is true of the Christian family is also true potentially for the entire human family. Think of it this way: for love to exist, three things must be one — a lover; the beloved whom the lover loves; and the love that together, they share. This is the minimum requirement for love to exist completely. Together, the two analogies we have from the human person help us see that the unity-in-distinction of the three Persons of the Trinity is imaged within the human soul and through the procession of love that exists within a family. Thus, it is reasonable to say that if *God is love*, the Trinity of Persons within God is necessary. One thing to keep in mind, however, is that the Church does not teach that the Father and the Holy Spirit are husband and wife, who together give rise to a Son. Rather, we believe that the Holy Spirit proceeds as the love shared in common by the Father and the Son. The analogy thus works in the other direction. A husband and wife and their children form a communion of love that images who God is as Father, Son, and Spirit.

Together, the four analogies we have considered give a strong indication that the Christian belief in one God who is three Persons is not unreasonable or impossible. Yet let us now look precisely at how the Church defines the doctrine of the Trinity. The *Catechism* states, "In order to articulate the dogma of the Trinity, the Church had to develop her own terminology with the help of certain notions of philosophical origin" (251). Using these philosophical concepts, the Church teaches that God exists as three Persons who together share one *nature* and *essence*. In *substance*, each Person of the Trinity is the same Divine Being: "We do not confess three Gods, but one God in three persons.... The divine persons do not share the one divinity among themselves but each of them is God whole and entire: 'The Father is that which the Son is, the Son that which the Father is, the Father and the Son that which the Holy Spirit is, i.e. by nature one God'" (CCC 253).

The doctrine of the Trinity explained

To speak of one God as three Persons is an especially strange way to speak, so let us see what this means by looking at what the notion of *person* actually means when we are speaking about God. We are accustomed to thinking of a person as a separate and distinct individual. Because of this, it is easy to think that each Person in the Trinity is a separate and distinct god. However, this is not what the Church means when she uses the term *person* to describe God. In God, the three Persons exist not as individual substances but because of four relationships that exist in the one God.

The first is the Source of the Godhead, the One "from whom" the other relations in God originate. Jesus called that Source the *Father* (John 14). God the Father refers to the Person within the Godhead "from whom" the Eternal Word proceeds. The Eternal Word is the second relationship within the Godhead. The Eternal Word is God's knowledge of himself, as in Augustine's psychological analogy explained above. The Gospel of John tells us that the Word of God is the *Son* of God. Here is how St. John describes it in his Gospel: "In the beginning was the Word, and the Word was with God, and the Word was God. He was in the beginning with God.... And the Word became flesh and dwelt among us, full of grace and truth; we have beheld his glory, glory as of the only Son from the Father" (1:1–2, 14). The Son is called "son" because he bears the image of the Father. The Father is called "father" because he eternally begets the son.

The Son is thus "begotten" of the Father as the Eternal Word and as a perfect image of the Father. While the difference is greater than the similarity, think about how a human father begets a human son, who bears his image. The difference is this: because the Word is *eternally* begotten, the Son has no beginning or end, just like the Father. The Source eternally generates the Word, and thus the Persons of the Father and the Son exist only as (and never apart from) an eternal relationship to each other. To help you think about this, imagine an eternal sun generating everlasting light. The Father is the Eternal Father because he exists in relation to his eternally begotten Son — as Christians profess in the Creed: "God from God, light from light, true God from true God, begotten, not made, consubstantial [of one substance] with the Father."

The first two *relationships* are thus Fatherhood and Sonship. Yet what about the other two, and where does the Holy Spirit fit in? Because the Father and the Son are in an eternal relationship "with" each other, as the Gospel of John states, the Father and the Son also share in common an Eternal Love. Thus, the third and fourth relationships are the Father's love for the Son and the Son's love for the Father. This *Eternal Love* is the Third Person of the Trinity; he proceeds from the Father and the Son together as the spirit of their love. This is how the Church explains it: "'Father,' 'Son,' 'Holy Spirit' are not simply names designating modalities of the divine being, for they are really distinct from one another.... They are distinct from one another in their relations of origin: 'It is the Father who generates, the Son who is begotten, and the Holy Spirit who proceeds [as love]'" (CCC 254).

Keep in mind, again, what I said above, that love requires three distinct things that are one—a lover, a beloved, and the love they share. In God, each of these three is a Divine Person. Remember, too, that divine love is not sexual, because there are no bodies involved in this exchange. This eternal procession of love is rooted in a completely spiritual procession. Thus, the Father gives everything he is to the Son; the Son gives everything he is to the Father; and that which they give is their love for each other. *This is who God is in Himself.* This is the deepest mystery of the Christian Faith: that *being* exists as an eternal procession of love and gift, and that God made humankind in his image and likeness. The *Catechism* sums up the doctrine of the Trinity like this: "The divine persons are relative to one another. Because it does not divide the divine unity, the real distinction of the persons from one another resides solely in the relationships which relate them to one another ... 'While they are called three persons in view of their relations, we believe in one nature or substance.' Indeed 'everything (in them) is one where there is no opposition of relationship'" (255).

The God of Jesus Christ

The Trinity is a great mystery, but what it means is that the great I AM who revealed himself to Moses is an eternal communion of three Divine Persons. Moreover, God has shared his inner life with us through the Incarnation of the Son, the Word of God, who has become a human being in the person of Jesus Christ.

Is God male?

Before ending this chapter, let me consider a couple more things. When speaking about God, one might tend to associate each Person of the Trinity with a different role or function. For example, Christians commonly speak of the Father as the Creator, the Son as the Redeemer, and the Spirit as the Sanctifier. In the economy of salvation, this is an accurate way to speak about God's deeds. However, to keep in mind that each Person of the Trinity is involved in all the works of God is also important. The Father creates in word and love. The Son redeems in the name of the Father and in the power of the Holy Spirit. The Spirit sanctifies through the Father's Word. Do you get the idea? The Trinity is completely one in substance and at work; thus, the distinction of Persons is only in respect to the relationships I described above.

Throughout this chapter and within the teachings of the Church generally, you will also notice that the Church refers to God in the masculine—with pronouns such as he, him, or his. The reason for this is not that God is a gender-specific being. God is not male or female, although the second Person of the Trinity did assume a male human nature. In fact, we believe God possesses all the characteristics of masculinity and femininity perfectly within himself (see CCC 239). The reason for the masculine pronouns, therefore, is that Jesus reveals that he is the Divine Son of an Eternal Father. It would not make sense to refer to this relationship in the feminine. Second, in relationship to creation, the masculine pronoun speaks to God's transcendent nature and his role as the (paternal) source of creation. God conceives creation's existence outside his being. God is not part of creation but is completely distinct from it. Just as new human life emerges outside a man's body, and within a woman's body, so creation does not originate from within God's nature, as though God were a generative mother.

Another way to think of it is to say that creation proceeds from the heart of God as a beloved spouse, but outside of God's nature — as, by analogy, Eve proceeds as a distinct creature from the side of Adam in the Book of Genesis (2:21–22). Consequently, this is also why the Judeo-Christian tradition uses the feminine pronoun in reference to the earth and the Church. Natural and supernatural life emerge from within creation and from within the Church, by the action of God's Word. By God's "fatherhood," the Word causes creation and the Church to become maternal — that is, life-bearing. By the nuptial union of the uncreated power of God and the created order, new life comes to be. We will look more closely at the doctrine of creation in the next two chapters. There I will explain more fully the reasons Scripture describes God's relationship to creation, and especially to humankind, as a spousal (nuptial) relationship.

9

The Creator of Heaven and Earth

In the last chapter, I ended by looking at why Christians call God *Father*. From the doctrine of the Trinity, Christians believe that the first Person, the Eternal Father, is primarily Father of the Eternal Son. More evidently, even to other religious traditions, God is also Father to the whole of creation. For a Christian to say, "I believe in one God, the Father almighty, maker of heaven and earth," as professed in the Nicene Creed, is to say that God brought the whole of creation into existence. As the psalmist declares, "By the word of the Lord the heavens were made, and all their host by the breath of his mouth" (Ps. 33:6).

The primary source of the Christian understanding of the doctrine of creation comes from the book of Genesis and the wisdom literature of the Old Testament. As the *Catechism* teaches,

> Among all the Scriptural texts about creation, the first three chapters of Genesis occupy a unique place ... The inspired authors have placed them at the beginning of Scripture to express in their solemn language the truths of creation — its origin and its end in God, its order and goodness, the vocation of man, and finally the drama of sin and the hope of salvation ... These texts remain the principal source for

catechesis on the mysteries of the "beginning": creation, fall, and promise of salvation. (289)

The Church teaches that the work of creation is that of the entire Trinity, and not just the Father. The first verses of Genesis hint at the creative work of the Trinity in a poetic, but subtle way: "The earth was without form and void, and darkness was upon the face of the deep; and the Spirit of God was moving over the face of the waters. Then God said, 'Let there be light'; and there was light" (1:2–3). In this first act of creation, the Father is the source of all creation and he creates through his Word: "All things were made through him, and without him was not anything made that was made" (John 1:3). The Holy Spirit, whom Christians profess in the Creed to be the "Lord, the giver of life," is also present as the wind hovering over the waters, disposing the earth to receive the creative power of the Father's Word.

God created all things from nothing

As we saw in a previous chapter, God is entirely distinct from cre-ation—that is, God is not the universe or any part of it, and the universe is not divine. Based on this truth, Christians believe that God created the universe out of nothing (*ex nihilo*). Although the Trinity is intimately involved in creating everything, God did not make the cosmos out of himself or from any preexisting matter. From nothing, he brought into being the existence of all things that once did not exist. "By faith we understand that the world was created by the word of God, so that what is seen was made out of things which do not appear" (Heb. 11:3). By implication, before the creation of the universe, there was nothing whatsoever except the Holy Trinity, not even time.

The creation of the universe from nothing is significant for our understanding of the cosmos. First, it means that creation is not eternal but exists within time and is finite and corruptible. While creation may continue infinitely into the future, it definitely had a beginning. Strangely enough, this was not something the philosophers of old, such as Aristotle, could prove. Ancients thought that matter was eternal, along with the gods. Even today, some scientists maintain that the universe is an infinite cycle of life and death, expansion and contraction. Some even believe in a multiverse—the reality of many simultaneous universes that come and go forever. However, with the discovery of the big bang and the assistance of quantum physics, we now can prove scientifically that the universe (or possible multiverses) had a definite beginning. What is amazing about the discovery of the big bang is that all the possibilities and potential for the entire cosmos began as one absolute and condensed singularity.[7]

That God created everything from nothing also suggests that the universe is entirely dependent upon God, who designed and sustains every creature and system of created existence. The Church teaches that "drawn from nothingness by God's power, wisdom and goodness, [a creature] can do nothing if it is cut off from its origin, for 'without a Creator the creature vanishes.' Still less can a creature attain its ultimate end without the help of God's grace" (CCC 308). While every creature has its own particular being and internal principles of development, nothing is completely autonomous in its existence, but everything participates in God's being. *Participation* means that at every moment of its existence, every creature derives its being from God—that is, the power of every creature subsists by God's existence. By way of metaphor,

---

[7] If you are a scientifically minded person, I would encourage you to read a book by Fr. Robert Spitzer, S.J., called *New Proofs for the Existence of God: Contributions of Contemporary Physics and Philosophy* (Grand Rapids, MI: Eerdmans, 2010). In it, he discusses how modern physics helps prove that the universe had a beginning and needs a Creator to account for itself.

think of how an electronic device has no operation apart from its power source. The power source and the device are distinct but intrinsically connected to each other.

The providence of God

Because of creation's dependency on God, Christians believe that the hand of divine providence has guided creation's development into an unimaginable multiplicity of creatures, in all of their various dimensions, natures, forms, and relationships. Over billions of years, creation has emerged gradually into an incredibly complex, beautiful, and interdependent community of being. "Creation ... did not spring forth complete from the hands of the Creator. The universe was created 'in a state of journeying' (*in statu viae*) toward an ultimate perfection yet to be attained, to which God has destined it. We call 'divine providence' the dispositions by which God guides his creation toward this perfection" (CCC 302).

Every system within the cosmos — be it microscopic or galactic in scale — is delicately tuned and perfectly ordered down to the last detail. Is this an accident? Every creature is integrated so seamlessly with everything else that it sounds ridiculous to Christian sensibilities that the universe could have happened randomly without God, or that the cosmos could have brought itself into existence and ordered itself. To us who indeed know so little about the cosmos, things might appear to be happenstance. Nevertheless, Christians believe the cosmos is sustained and governed in every instance by the providence of God, who has "arranged all things by measure and number and weight" (Wisd. 11:20). This is how the Church describes divine providence:

We believe that God created the world according to his wisdom. It is not the product of any necessity whatever, nor of blind fate or chance. We believe that it proceeds from God's free will; he wanted to make his creatures share in his being, wisdom and goodness: "For you created all things, and by your will they existed and were created." Therefore, the psalmist exclaims: "O LORD, how manifold are your works! In wisdom you have made them all"; and "The LORD is good to all, and his compassion is over all that he has made." ... God does not abandon his creatures to themselves. He not only gives them being and existence, but also, and at every moment, upholds and sustains them in being, enables them to act and brings them to their final end [perfection]. (CCC 295, 301)

Creation is thus a perpetual work of God's love and imagination.

Yet according to the Christian Faith, God does not do all the work of creation on his own. He has imparted to the whole of creation the means of its own growth and development:

God is the sovereign master of his plan. But to carry it out he also makes use of his creatures' co-operation. This use is not a sign of weakness, but rather a token of almighty God's greatness and goodness. For God grants his creatures not only their existence, but also the dignity of acting on their own, of being causes and principles for each other, and thus of co-operating in the accomplishment of his plan. (CCC 306)

A more contemporary way to say this is that God is not a micromanager. He allows creation to share in his glory by allowing each creature to have its own shared glory.

The Creator of all that is visible and invisible

When we consider *what* God created, Christians know by faith and, to some extent, by reason that God created two orders, or realms—the visible and the invisible. The *invisible* order includes all angelic beings, which Genesis says God created first, when he created light (1:3). Christian tradition maintains that the light referenced on the first day refers to the creation of the angels, because the text states that God did not create the stars until the fourth day (Gen. 1:14). Prior to the creation of the stars, God separated the light and darkness, suggesting that the war among the angels and the fall of Satan occurred prior to the creation of the visible order (Gen 1:4; Rev. 12). We do not know a lot about the angels, but here is how the *Catechism* describes them:

> As purely *spiritual* creatures angels have intelligence and will: they are personal and immortal creatures, surpassing in perfection all visible creatures, as the splendor of their glory bears witness.... With their whole beings the angels are *servants* and messengers of God ... Christ is the center of the angelic world. They are *his* angels.... They belong to him because they were created *through* and *for* him: "for in him all things were created in heaven and on earth, visible and invisible, whether thrones or dominions or principalities or authorities." ... They belong to him still more because he has made them messengers of his saving plan. (330, 329, 331)

Because they are pure spirits, we cannot see angels unless they appear to us as visions. While most people are familiar with the story of the Angel Gabriel appearing to the Virgin Mary, one of the most explicit descriptions of an angel in Scripture comes from the book of Tobit. In it, we hear the Archangel Raphael describe who and what he is:

> "Now when you, Tobit, and Sarah prayed, it was I who presented the record of your prayer before the Glory of the Lord; and likewise whenever you used to bury the dead.

When you did not hesitate to get up and leave your dinner in order to go and bury that dead man, I was sent to put you to the test. At the same time, however, God sent me to heal you and your daughter-in-law Sarah. I am Raphael, one of the seven angels who stand and serve before the Glory of the Lord." Greatly shaken, the two of them fell prostrate in fear. But Raphael said to them: "Do not fear; peace be with you! Bless God now and forever. As for me, when I was with you, I was not acting out of any favor on my part, but by God's will. So bless God every day; give praise with song. Even though you saw me eat and drink, I did not eat or drink anything; what you were seeing was a vision. So now bless the Lord on earth and give thanks to God. Look, I am ascending to the one who sent me. Write down all that has happened to you." And he ascended. They stood up but were no longer able to see him. (12:12–21, NABRE)

Besides the angelic world of pure spirit, the *invisible* order also includes the human spirit. Human beings are not mere animals comprised of matter, although it might seem like it.

The Christian Faith maintains that the human soul has a spiritual and thus immaterial nature that surpasses the material souls of plants and other animals. Even according to the ancient philosophers, such as Aristotle and Plato, all plants and animals have souls—a principle of animation or life—but only humankind has a spiritual soul that lives forever after God creates it (see CCC 362–367). Yet we inhabit a visible and material order as our principal mode of existence. The *visible* order includes the whole of space and all the billions of galaxies that exist. The expanse of the visible universe is incomprehensible to our minds in its breadth. The visible order includes all the elements and minerals we see under the microscope, as well as the stellar bodies we see in space. Within this celestial landscape exists, at least on this little planet, a full spectrum of biological reality, from microbes to the giant blue whale.

As the narrative of Genesis 1 explains by using the symbolic account of the six days of creation, God arranged the cosmos hierarchically. This means that some creatures are closer to God in their resemblance of him than others are. The pinnacle of the visible order is the creation of personal beings — the human family — who bear God's image to the highest degree (CCC 342–343). The hierarchy of being also suggests that God made the lower creatures for the higher creatures. For example, the elements form the building blocks of biological life. Higher biological forms assimilate lower ones by eating them, while animals assimilate all of these into sentient life. Ultimately, spiritual existence assimilates material existence through the body, as we see in the example of human life, which is composed of matter and spirit.

While Genesis does describe this hierarchy of consumption and assimilation, the text primarily describes the hierarchy of being in terms of the dominion that different creatures have over different realms — for instance, the fish over the sea, the birds over the air, the cattle over the fields, and humanity over the whole of the earth (Gen. 1). The implication of God's providential care for this beautifully ordered, hierarchically arranged universe is that everything God has made is loved and given as a gift (Gen. 1:28 –31). God loves creation, and he wills that everything exist and flourish under the stewardship of the human race:

> Our human understanding, which shares in the light of the divine intellect, can understand what God tells us by means of his creation, though not without great effort and only in a spirit of humility and respect before the Creator and his work. Because creation comes forth from God's goodness, it shares in that goodness — "And God saw that it was good

… very good"—for God willed creation as a gift addressed to man, an inheritance destined for and entrusted to him. (CCC 299)

Ultimately, all things have been made subject to the human race—even the angels—through the Incarnation of Jesus Christ. This means that Jesus was, ultimately, whom God had in mind when he created everything in the beginning, through his Son and for his Son (see Col. 1:15–20).

In the light of the love God has for creation, and because every creature is a gift of God, Christians profess that creation is made for the glory of God. At first, this sounds selfish on God's part, but the Church means something quite different than we might think. As St. Bonaventure (1221–1274) said, "God created all things 'not to increase his glory, but to show it forth and to communicate it,' for God has no other reason for creating than his love and goodness" (quoted in CCC 293). In other words, the purpose for which God created everything in such perfect order and beauty was so that creation could share in the glory and goodness of its Creator by means of the Incarnation of God's Word in the Person of Jesus Christ. This is why Jesus declares, "I am the Alpha and the Omega, the first and the last, the beginning and the end" (Rev. 22:13).

The theory of evolution and modern cosmology

In recent times, the greatest challenges to the doctrine of creation have arisen from the theory of evolution and certain theories of quantum physics. Some scientists, for example, argue that modern scientific discoveries contradict the book of Genesis and that the biblical accounts are therefore unreliable. As we have seen already, the book of Genesis is not attempting to give a scientific account of the origins of the universe. No contradiction exists between the truths of reason and the truths of faith. Rather, Genesis speaks to important religious and philosophical insights, such as God's creation of all things from nothing, the order and goodness of creation, and the reflection of God's image in all creatures.

The Church teaches that the theory of evolution and some of the cosmological arguments from modern physics pose no problem to faith, so long as Christians reject some of the philosophical claims such scientific theories propose. For example, Christians reject that the big bang was a random occurrence—and science cannot prove that it was, or that the age of the universe is infinite. In fact, these are actually philosophically untenable claims at this point. Another big challenge has been the philosophical assertion of some evolutionary biologists that natural selection proves that we do not need God to explain the origin and development of species. Scientific theories are wonderful for explaining the material causes of the universe—what we might call the "mechanics" of the atomic, physical, chemical, and biological processes that comprise the operations of the created order. However, these methods are limited to these considerations alone and do not prove that God does not exist or that God is not intimately involved in the ongoing work of creation.

The Christian doctrine of creation does not displace the discoveries of science but helps those discoveries find their greater context and spiritual significance. The perennial theological question is this: why does anything exist in the first place, and for what purpose? Why is there a universe at all, and how did it get here? Sacred Scripture helps us understand the answers to these questions. Just because the language of Scripture is figurative and poetic does not mean it does not speak truthfully about the nature of creation and the Creator. The sciences do not refute what we believe in faith, but only help us appreciate the majesty of our Creator even more. The more we discover, the greater should be our praise! The book of Sirach makes just such an acclamation: "There is One who is wise, greatly to be feared, sitting upon his throne. The Lord himself created wisdom; he saw her and apportioned her, he poured her out upon all his works. She dwells with all flesh according to his gift, and he supplied her to those who love him" (1:8–10). In fact, the wisdom literature reminds us that praise is always the best response to the spellbinding wonderment and beauty of creation.

As a final consideration, when we reflect upon the whole of what Scripture tells us about creation, it leaves us with a profound realization, that the works of creation are the *liturgy* (meaning "works") that God performs on behalf of his beloved creatures. As we will see in the next chapter, God created the universe primarily as a place of communion and worship for the angels and the human race. In the biblical mindset, liturgy and worship always take place in a temple. In our scientific mentality today, the stage God has constructed fascinates us, but we forget about the drama played out on that stage. Our fixation on technical knowledge and conquering the order of creation, as opposed to simply marveling at the One who created it, is like spending our entire existence trying to understand our house without paying attention to the family life that unfolds within its walls. In the next chapter, we will consider the drama of human existence that has unfolded within the holy temple of God's creation.

10

The Story of Adam and Eve

The creation narratives in the first three chapters of Genesis reveal to us many important truths, even if these truths are not of a "scientific" nature. Biblical truth sheds a light on the nature of many things quite important to human existence. As we saw in the last chapter, the creation narratives help us grasp that God created the world out of love and gave it an order that reflects his infinite wisdom. This is why God declares after each stage that creation "is good." In poetic language, Genesis tells us that God created the invisible world of the angels (the light) and then the visible world of earthly creatures. God created different realms, and then he created creatures to govern those realms.

At the end of the sixth day of creation, God made the human race in his image and likeness and gave us dominion over the earth to care for God's visible creation as its stewards. This is the biblical meaning of having *dominion* (CCC 373). At the center of this story are the first parents of the human race — Adam and Eve. The biblical authors intended these names to be symbolic. *Adam* means "man" and could be rendered "from the earth," while *Eve* could mean "life," as Adam calls her "mother of all living" (Gen. 3:20). As mentioned previously, we now know scientifically that all *Homo sapiens* are genetically related by a single point of origin, which again indicates that the biblical account of an original couple is not pure myth but is borne out by modern science.

God created a cosmic temple

In order to convey the deepest significance of the Adam and Eve narratives, however, the Church teaches that the biblical authors intended to narrate the creation of a cosmic temple (see CCC 347). We know this from other writings of the Old Testament, where it becomes clear that the Temple Solomon built in Jerusalem was a miniature replica of the entire universe. Within the Temple precincts, the architects represented all of the different aspects of creation — the Garden, the seas, the constellations, and all the precious metals and gems ancient peoples extracted from the earth (1 Kings 6–8; 1 Chron. 28; 2 Chron. 3–5). The Temple even had a zoo and a botanical garden that, together, represented all the different species of life. The Temple was a *microcosmos*, which means that in the religious imagination of the Jewish people, the universe was a cosmic temple (see CCC 1145–1151).

At the heart of the Temple in Jerusalem was a chamber called the *Holy of Holies*. Only the high priest of Israel entered this space once a year for a sacrifice. God instructed Israel to adorn the veil leading into the Holy of Holies as a garden. The Holy of Holies was the sacred space where God dwelt among the people of Israel. It housed the Ark of the Covenant, which held the Ten Commandments and several other sacred objects of the Old Covenant. The spiritual meaning of the Temple in Jerusalem helps us understand the deepest meaning of the creation narrative from Genesis — that the world is a holy temple.

If Genesis 1 tells us that the world is a temple, Genesis 2 describes the Garden as the Holy of Holies, with the priest-king (Adam) and the queen mother of all humanity (Eve). The two chapters are thus one continuous narrative. Together with God, Adam and Eve live in the Garden sanctuary as rulers of the earth. The command to "till and keep [the Garden]" is actually a phrase that has priestly and liturgical connotations (Gen. 2:15). While not meant to be a scientific account of creation, Genesis offers a beautiful revelation about the deepest meaning of creation, as well as the role of the human family within the house God built from nothing (*ex nihilo*).

The significance of Adam and Eve

The primary purpose of the Adam and Eve narratives, therefore, is to distinguish the human family from all the other visible creatures of the earth and to reveal our vocation as creatures called into being for love and worship. This is the deepest significance of bearing God's image and likeness. The human race is the "summit of the Creator's work" (CCC 343). God created humankind to act as mediators (priests) between God and the rest of creation. Through humanity, God desires to bless creation with his grace. Through us, all creation finds a voice of praise and thanksgiving to God.

If we look a little more deeply into the Adam and Eve story, we discover other beautiful and profound truths about the human race. As we will consider in the next chapter, human beings are unique because we are a combination of both the invisible and visible realms of the created order, a composite of body and spirit (CCC 362). Together, the body and soul form a single substance of embodied personhood. The soul does not *inhabit* the body; rather, the soul is the actual cause of the life and spiritual existence *of* the body. Not only are human beings material beings within the visible order, but also we have a spiritual and rational soul, which animates matter and gives the material order the power and experience of consciousness. The *Catechism* states, "The unity of soul and body is so profound that one has to consider the soul to be the 'form' of the body: i.e., it is because of its spiritual soul that the body made of matter becomes a living, human body; spirit and matter, in man, are not two natures united, but rather their union forms a single nature" (365).

From a Christian perspective, the reason this is important is that humankind is not mere stardust—a purely material being—or some random occurrence in a heartless and meaningless universe. Our existence matters terribly to the whole of God's relationship with the visible realm. Consciousness gives humanity the ability to reason, to love, and to experience God and the world around us in a personal and intimate way. Consciousness gives us the capacity for worship—communion with God in truth and love (see CCC 347). The *Catechism* tells us, "God created everything for man, but man in turn was created to serve and love God and to offer all creation back to him" (358).

As embodied spirits, human beings thus enjoy a special privilege. As mysterious as this may seem, every human being is a microcosmos, a universe in miniature—just like the Jerusalem Temple. Each of us is comprised of every aspect of the created order—matter and spirit—which might explain why Psalm 8 declares:

> When I see your heavens, the work of your fingers, the moon and stars that you set in place—what is man that you are mindful of him, and a son of man that you care for him? Yet you have made him little less than a god, crowned him with glory and honor. You have given him rule over the works of your hands, put all things at his feet. (4–7, NABRE)

The psalmist is praising God for the incredible dignity of the human race, which God established as the priestly stewards over all creation. If every human person is a microcosmos, each human person is also a temple of God; each of us is a place for God to dwell. This is why St. Paul, when exhorting Christian disciples to safeguard their purity, asks, "Do you not know that your body is a temple of the Holy Spirit within you, which you have from God? You are not your own" (1 Cor. 6:19).

The Adam and Eve story also provides other significant truths about the meaning of human existence. God walked upon the earth in the Garden of Eden (Gen. 3:8). This symbolically describes a primordial time of innocence and intimacy with God, which was disrupted by the first sin. We learn that God gave humanity his grace by breathing his Spirit into Adam and Eve (Gen. 2:7). "By the radiance of this grace all dimensions of man's life were confirmed. As long as he remained in the divine intimacy, man would not have to suffer or die" (CCC 376). The grace God gave was a participation in the divine nature, by which God made Adam and Eve his children. As the *Catechism* states, "This grace of original holiness was 'to share in ... divine life'" (CCC 375). If there had been other human-like creatures on earth at the time, as anthropologists claim, *Homo sapiens* would have stood apart, because God gave humankind supernatural gifts and directed our lives toward Heaven, which is symbolized by the Tree of Life in the center of the Garden of Eden (Gen. 2:9).

Original innocence, unity, and justice

Another way the Church speaks about original holiness is in reference to Adam and Eve's state of *original justice*. This means that God created our first parents without sin, flaws, or weaknesses, aside from the natural vulnerabilities of being a creature. Adam and Eve experienced within themselves a four-fold unity. In the beginning, their hearts were joined in love to God, and their minds adhered to all the truths by which they could remain in God's fellowship. Because of this union of their souls with God, their bodies were subject to their souls, giving their bodies an immortal quality capable of resisting the natural corruption of the flesh. In other words, had they not sinned, they would not have experienced physical degeneration and death. God warns them that if they ate of the Tree the Knowledge of Good and Evil, they would die (Gen. 2:17). Had they persevered in faith, the blessedness of Heaven would have remained open to them; instead, their sin exiled them from paradise and intimacy with God.

The third experience of unity Adam and Eve enjoyed was with each other. Lust did not mar their relationship, and they enjoyed a perfect marital friendship. Genesis describes this as the experience of nakedness without shame (2:25). Finally, in their state of original innocence, Adam and Eve experienced a perfect dominion over the earth. They could exercise their dominion over creation with great responsibility and care as a perfect reflection of God's providential love over all he had created. In summary, the *Catechism* explains:

> The Church, interpreting the symbolism of biblical language in an authentic way, in the light of the New Testament and Tradition, teaches that our first parents, Adam and Eve, were constituted in an original "state of holiness and justice." This grace of original holiness was "to share in … divine life." By the radiance of this grace all dimensions of man's life were confirmed. As long as he remained in the divine intimacy, man would not have to suffer or die. The inner harmony of the human person, the harmony between man and woman, and finally the harmony between the first couple and all creation, comprised the state called "original justice." (375–376)

This fourfold harmony was the basis of peace and represented an original innocence that would have remained, had Adam and Eve not sinned.

The Story of Adam and Eve

God reveals his grand plan, a great mystery of love and redemption

The Adam and Eve story also reveals important truths about human sexuality and marital union. Besides the wonderful union Adam and Eve enjoyed with God, they experienced the mystery of their innocence in the distinction and generosity of their sexuality. God created humanity male and female (Gen. 1:27). Together, through the mutual exchange of their love and friendship, not only could Adam and Eve, as one, attain a likeness to God's inner life of love and communion, but they could also become fruitful in their love through children, as God is fruitful in his love through creating the universe (see CCC 293). By binding themselves to one another as one flesh, through the wonder of their marital union and in accordance with God's command to "be fruitful and multiply," man and woman could bring forth new life free of disordered sexual desire; without pain or sorrow; and in a manner altogether distinct from that of the other animals, namely, as the expression of freedom and love (Gen. 1:28). This is the deepest meaning and vocation of human sexuality (see CCC 369–373).

God also assigned equal value and dignity to Adam and Eve and called them to live "for each other" in communion with God. This is the meaning of Adam's words when he looked upon Eve for the first time: "This at last is bone of my bones and flesh of my flesh" (Gen. 2:23). In the state of original justice, the man did not disparage the woman or view her as subservient. Each had a mutual regard and respect for the other. This also is what the narrative means when it states that Adam and Eve were both naked, but they experienced no shame. They did not look upon one another as an object of use but as a gift from the hand of the Creator.

The fact that the Bible begins with a marital union between Adam and Eve is significant too. After God created Eve and presented her to Adam, the text states, "Therefore a man leaves his father and his mother and cleaves to his wife, and they become one flesh" (Gen. 2:24). In the liturgical context of the creation narratives described above, we can discern that the entire act of creation and the union of God with creation through the Incarnation of the Word, Jesus Christ, reveal that the primal event that occurs within the cosmic temple of creation is a nuptial union between Heaven and earth, between God and the whole of creation. The creation of Adam and Eve, and their becoming one flesh, signifies a great mystery. As St Paul tells us, referencing Genesis,

> For no one hates his own flesh but rather nourishes and cherishes it, even as Christ does the church, because we are members of his body. "For this reason a man shall leave [his] father and [his] mother and be joined to his wife, and the two shall become one flesh." This is a great mystery, but I speak in reference to Christ and the church. In any case, each one of you should love his wife as himself, and the wife should respect her husband. (Eph. 5:29–32, NABRE)

The great mystery of which Paul speaks is the holy union of Christ and the people of God — the New Adam and his Body, the Church. When read in light of the whole of Scripture, the Adam and Eve story actually prefigures (foreshadows) Jesus, whom the Eternal Father has anointed as High Priest-King, and the Church, which is the mother of a new creation.

While on earth, Jesus described himself as the Bridegroom. John the Baptist echoed this language: "He who has the bride is the bridegroom; the friend of the bridegroom [John the Baptist] ... rejoices greatly at the bridegroom's voice" (John 3:29). The *Catechism* explains this relationship like this:

> The unity of Christ and the Church, head and members of one Body, also implies the distinction of the two within a personal relationship. This aspect is often expressed by

the image of bridegroom and bride. The theme of Christ as Bridegroom of the Church was prepared for by the prophets and announced by John the Baptist. The Lord referred to himself as the "bridegroom." The Apostle speaks of the whole Church and of each of the faithful, members of his Body, as a bride "betrothed" to Christ the Lord so as to become but one spirit with him. The Church is the spotless bride of the spotless Lamb. "Christ loved the Church and gave himself up for her, that he might sanctify her." He has joined her with himself in an everlasting covenant and never stops caring for her as for his own body. (CCC 796)

The Bible ends with a marriage as well—the wedding feast of the Lamb (Rev. 22:17). This is the consummation of the great plan of God's work of creation—a great marriage between Christ and the Church.

The point is that the creation account of Adam and Eve in Genesis prefigures the great plan of God to fashion from his divine heart a bride and join himself eternally to creation in a holy union of love. Adam signifies the bridegroom to come in Jesus; Eve signifies the bride—a holy people joined to God for eternity in Christ. Adam and Eve's actual union is thus so important because God's holy people have actually descended from their marital union.

Tragically, however, we know from Genesis 3 that Adam and Eve did not remain in the communion of God's love. Our first parents did not fulfill their vocation to love. Genesis 3 speaks about a forbidden tree. The Tree of the Knowledge of Good and Evil symbolizes the inherent limits of human freedom (CCC 396). While humanity is perfectly capable of discerning good from evil and acting accordingly, we do not have the authority to decide for ourselves what *is* good and evil. Genesis reveals that such authority belongs to God alone. He created everything and established the conditions for the perfection and complete happiness of every creature (CCC 301). By abusing their freedom, Adam and Eve sinned against God and brought tragic consequences upon the human family, which we will consider in another chapter.

Thankfully, the story does not end there. The most important truth we learn from the Adam and Eve story and the rest of Scripture, in fact, is that God had a plan to fix the mess Adam and Eve made. God has not abandoned the human race, and he has fulfilled his plan to redeem us through establishing covenants and, finally, in sending his Son, Jesus, to us. Scripture testifies that there is no evil so great that God's love cannot conquer it. In Genesis 3:15, we learn of a prophecy about God's defeat of Satan, the enemy of God and humanity. The *Catechism* explains, "The Christian tradition sees in this passage an announcement of the 'New Adam' who, because he 'became obedient unto death, even death on a cross,' makes amends superabundantly for the disobedience of Adam" (411). We learn further that a descendant of Eve will crush the serpent's head and defeat Satan.

The creation narratives do not reveal these essential truths about humanity's creation according to the methods of modern science or history. They speak powerfully and poetically about the deepest realities of human existence. They explain why we have great dignity and value, and they solve the riddle of the meaning and purpose of human existence. These stories tell us of our origins and God's promise to liberate us from the bondage of evil—that we might live forever in the eternal communion of his love as God's everlasting people and spouse.

11

The Dignity of Human Life

Since the dawn of history, human beings have wondered about the meaning of life. Philosophers have traditionally posed the question as "What is man?" Most people, in the course of their lives, also tangle themselves up with other questions about human existence. What happens after we die? Why do we suffer? Do our lives really matter? In one respect, these questions are natural to us because we are rational beings. The technical term for our species is *Homo sapiens*, which comes from the Latin for "man" (*homo*) and "wise" or "capable of discerning" (*sapiens*). Therefore, *Homo sapiens* literally means "wise or thinking man." Scientists actually distinguish humans from other animals by describing us as the "thinking primate." We stand on two feet in an upright position with our faces gazing upward at the stars. We are, quite literally, full of wonder.

However, given the expanse of the universe, is there anything all that special about us? Many people argue that humans are just material beings that occupy no significant place in the universe — mere stardust, like everything else. Some question if our evolution beyond other animals makes us more valuable than these other creatures. One of the most important contributions Judeo-Christian revelation has given to the world is the notion of human dignity. While philosophers of the ancient world understood that human beings possess a rational nature, it was not until the coming of Jesus Christ and the spread of the Christian gospel that people began to comprehend more fully the value of every human person beyond any distinction of race, sex, or social status.

In fact, Christians introduced the world to the concepts of personhood, human dignity, and human rights, as well as the ethical implications of the belief that God created humanity for friendship with himself and redeemed us after we fell into sin. Christianity has always professed that we are far more than dust or mere animals, as God has placed us above the world of matter—that we remain at the center of God's creative purposes. It was the belief in human dignity that changed the course of history and the moral landscape of law, by insisting that all human beings are beloved by God and, because of God's love for us, that he commands us to love one another.

Christians were the first to affirm the equal value of women and children, for example, and to abolish the practices of abortion and slavery. Christians limited the justification for war to self-defense and were the first to believe that marriage should proceed from the free choice of love. Christians invented universal education and hospitals.[8] While it is true that, through the centuries, many Christians have not lived up to Christian belief, the Scriptures give us the first clear theological indication about why we are different from other earthly creatures. The Church still professes these things to this day. Every person belongs to God, and we are to respect every person as having profound dignity, even the greatest of sinners and our enemies (Matt. 5:38–48). This is why Christians say we are "pro-life." We believe human life is sacred and inviolable

---

[8] You will find a good summary of all these accomplishments in a book by Thomas Woods, Jr., *How the Catholic Church Built Western Civilization* (Washington, DC: Regnery Publishing, 2005).

from conception to natural death. We belong to God alone, and he safeguards us by his love for us.

Dignity and the vocation of human personhood

What does it mean to have dignity? To have dignity means to be worthy of honor or respect — to possess great value and worth. To deny someone's dignity is to view and treat her as expendable or as something we can use and discard when it no longer serves a purpose. When we fail to see the dignity of another person, we look down upon him as someone or something we can ignore or disregard. What makes humanity special is that God created us as beings capable of forming relationships of love. To be able to do this, as we have seen already, God endowed man and woman with rational souls, that is, the powers of intellect and will, giving us the ability to know and understand the truth and to choose what is objectively good.

As the *Catechism* explains, "Being in the image of God the human individual ... is not just something, but someone. He is capable of self-knowledge, of self-possession and of freely giving himself and entering into communion with other persons. And he is called by grace to a covenant with his Creator, to offer him a response of faith and love that no other creature can give in his stead" (CCC 357). This capability of self-knowledge, self-possession, and freely giving oneself in love — whether we use it or not — means that a human being is some*one* rather than some*thing*; a *person* rather than just another animal.

The fact that God made us in his image and likeness is a bedrock of the Christian Faith. As we have seen already, Christians believe God is a communion of three Divine Persons, Father, Son, and Holy Spirit. To be made in God's image is to be made such that we can experience love as an integral part of our nature. We are capable of this because we have a rational soul that gives us the capacity for love. In fact, this is the meaning and purpose of human life—to experience the communion of love, first with God and then with each other. This is why having a rational soul is special and "that which is of greatest value" in us (CCC 363). No human being is without this value, regardless of race, nationality, sex, socioeconomic status, political affiliation, or behavior. Even the worst of sinners and the most disabled persons retain their dignity.

For God to create us in his image, then, suggests that he calls us into existence to live for the vocation of love—that is, to love and be loved—and for no other reason. As a vocation (a personal call), love is something we must freely give and receive. When we fulfill our vocation to love, we reflect the reality of who God is in himself and thus become *like* him. The *Catechism* explains, "The divine image is present in every man. It shines forth in the communion of persons, in the likeness of the unity of the divine persons among themselves. ... There is a certain resemblance between the unity of the divine persons and the fraternity that men are to establish among themselves in truth and love. Love of neighbor is inseparable from love for God" (1702, 1878).

Along with the soul, the human body also possesses tremendous dignity. The human body is not just mere matter but is animated by the soul and so becomes an integral part of the person. Scripture tells us, "The Lord God formed man of dust from ground, and breathed into his nostrils the breath of life; and man became a living being" (Gen. 2:7). This is why we believe we may never exploit the human body for the sake of personal gain or selfish enjoyment. Each person in the whole of his or her bodily existence belongs to God, who gives bodily and spiritual life to everyone. We are to revere the whole person by showing everyone the greatest respect, care, and honor. Some think it is okay to disregard the body by cheapening its value through various kinds of inappropriate pleasures and uses.

For Christians, God insists that we treat our bodies in a manner that respects his image and likeness.

The dignity of the human body is especially important when it comes to the complementarity of the two sexes, male and female. The *Catechism* explains,

> Man and woman have been *created*, which is to say, *willed* by God: on the one hand, in perfect equality as human persons; on the other, in their respective beings as man and woman. "Being man" or "being woman" is a reality which is good and willed by God: man and woman possess an inalienable dignity which comes to them immediately from God their Creator. Man and woman are both with one and the same dignity "in the image of God." In their "being-man" and "being-woman," they reflect the Creator's wisdom and goodness. (369)

God made us male and female, and he gave each the same dignity as human persons. He intended to distinguish humankind by the two sexes. Sexual distinction is not accidental or unessential to who a human person is.

God thus affirms the dignity of each sex and wills that each complements the other — that is, completes or makes one another perfect — in the communion of love. "Man and woman were made 'for each other' ... He created them to be a communion of persons, in which each can be 'helpmate' to the other, for they are equal as persons ... and complementary as masculine and feminine" (CCC 372). When a man and woman become husband and wife in marriage, they fully express this communion of love. Through this unique form of friendship, they share their bodies with one another for the sake of the unity of their life together, and, in the ordinary course of things, they create new life in cooperation with God's plan.

The Catholic Faith Explained

Jesus reveals human dignity

Christianity places such high value on the human person, body and soul, for another reason besides the image of God we bear. Essential to the Christian Faith is the truth that God assumed a human nature — body and soul — and in doing so, affirmed all that is human, with the exception of sin. We call this incredible gift the *Incarnation* — which literally means "made flesh." As we have seen already, the author of John's Gospel begins his testimony of Jesus — who is the Word of God — with this teaching: "And the Word became flesh and dwelt among us" (John 1:14). Without losing his divine nature, Jesus became fully human and experienced all that being human entails. He had human thoughts and temptations; he experienced emotions and bodily sensations. This can only mean that human beings are very dear to God. Otherwise, he would not have bothered to become one of us.

Not only did Jesus affirm human nature through the Incarnation, but in doing so, he also embodied the fullness of what it means to be human. "In reality it is only in the mystery of the Word made flesh that the mystery of man truly becomes clear" (CCC 359). Jesus showed us *how* to be human. Throughout the course of his earthly life, the Son of God taught us how to live and to love. He showed us that God made our souls for love and showed us how to love by offering his life — body and soul — on the Cross for our salvation. Instead of wielding his authority over us, Jesus made a gift of himself by sacrificing his life on behalf of ours. He freely shed his blood and experienced death so that we might have eternal life. As Jesus puts it, "Greater love has no man than this, that a man lay down his life for his friends" (John 15:13). His self-offering reveals to us what it means to be human — that not only do we possess great value, but we are also intended to love each other in the same way that he loves us (John 13:34).

The Dignity of Human Life

Our stewardship of creation

The fact that human beings enjoy such dignity does not mean that we have the right to disregard the importance and value of other creatures, however. Because we are persons made in God's image and likeness, we have a responsibility to care for all creatures and serve God as stewards of his creation. We do this properly when we treat other creatures according to the value they possess. As the *Catechism* explains, God commands us to have "respect for the integrity of creation. ... Man's dominion over inanimate and other living beings granted by the Creator is not absolute; it is limited by concern for the quality of life of his neighbor, including generations to come; it requires a religious respect for the integrity of creation" (2415). However, note that we care for creation not by treating other creatures as though they are human but by respecting the earth and all of its creatures as our common home.

In summary, revelation affirms the goodness of the human person — that we are wonderful creations and beloved by God. Christianity truly proclaims good news in a world where the dignity of the human person is increasingly threatened. Jesus Christ holds up to us the perfection of humankind. In him, we know our dignity and know how to treat one another as creatures made in the image and likeness of God, destined for everlasting life.

12

The Fall from Grace and the
Need for Redemption

In the last three chapters, as we looked at Genesis 1 and 2, we considered the wonderful works of God's creation. The crowning achievement of this work is the creation of our first parents as images of the trinitarian God and the high priestly stewards of the visible world. We learned about our vocation to love and God's plan of an eternal union of love with creation through the union of Christ and the Church. However, as we learn from the third chapter of Genesis, the sin of Adam and Eve profoundly disrupted God's original plan for the human family. Our first parents abused their freedom by disobeying God's command, and they lost their intimacy with God in the Garden of Eden. While the Church does not believe the first three chapters of Genesis give us a strictly "historical" account, "the account of the fall in Genesis 3 uses figurative language, but affirms a primeval event, a deed that took place at the beginning of the history of man" (CCC 390).

Genesis 3 introduces the demonic person of Satan, a fallen angel, who in the form of a serpent tempts our first parents to eat the fruit of the forbidden tree:

[The Serpent] asked the woman, "Did God really say, 'You shall not eat from any of the trees in the garden'?" The woman answered the snake: "We may eat of the fruit of the trees in the garden; it is only about the fruit of the tree in the middle of the garden that God said, 'You shall not eat it or even touch it, or else you will die.'" But the snake said to the woman: "You certainly will not die! God knows well that when you eat of it your eyes will be opened and you will be like gods, who know good and evil." (1–5, NABRE)

What happened at the dawn of human history was the loss of faith in God's love. This failure of trust led to the human sins of envy and pride—the desire to be gods by coveting God's gift of life rather receiving life and freedom as his gift to us. This is the same sin Satan committed. Our first parents preferred their own freedom to God's law of wisdom. "Man, tempted by the devil, let his trust in his Creator die in his heart and, abusing his freedom, disobeyed God's command" (CCC 397). Adam and Eve chose to walk by their own faulty judgment—and be deceived—rather than walk by the light of faith. The consequences were devastating. "After that first sin, the world is virtually inundated by sin" (CCC 401). What God perfectly ordered came largely unraveled by human failure.

The consequences of Original Sin

The four-fold harmony of original innocence, which we considered previously, disintegrated quickly as humans began to experience the effects of sin upon their lives. The *Catechism* describes this disintegration in stark terms:

The control of the soul's spiritual faculties over the body is shattered; the union of man and woman becomes subject to tensions, their relations henceforth marked by lust and domination. Harmony with creation is broken: visible creation has become alien and hostile to man. Because of man, creation is now subject "to its bondage to decay." Finally, the consequence explicitly foretold for this disobedience will come true: man will "return to the ground," for out of it he was taken. *Death makes its entrance into human history.* (400)

Let us take each one of these four "curses" and consider it individually. To begin, pride and envy isolated Adam and Eve from their intimacy with God, causing them to lose the grace by which they enjoyed their innocence and unity with God.

Adam and Eve broke the covenant God made with them by the fact that they rejected the truth of God's Word — his commands to them — and they selfishly willed their own pleasure before God's law. "The woman saw that the tree was good for food and pleasing to the eyes, and the tree was desirable for gaining wisdom" (Gen. 3:6, NABRE). They preferred their own judgment about what would bring them happiness over God's plan of happiness for them, a plan that required their obedience of faith. Their rejection of God's authority over their lives resulted in their expulsion from the Garden of Eden (the Holy of Holies), which had served as their paradise. This sin sets up a pattern for all time. Whenever we reject God's truth and put our own earthly pleasure — the satisfaction of our natural existence — before God's plan for our eternal happiness, we experience a great distance from God, and this is our own doing.

The second consequence of Original Sin follows directly from the first. Having rebelled against the divine wisdom, and without the grace of God operating within it, the human soul lost its power to preserve the body from its natural corruption. The separation of the soul from God leads directly to the separation of the body from the soul. The integrity of the body and soul thus degenerated through suffering and death. This second curse not only brings misery into the human experience of earthly life but also meant Adam and Eve had to face the reality that after death, they would have no access to Heaven. When God warns Adam and Eve not to eat the fruit of the forbidden tree, he tells them that if they do, they will die (Gen. 2:17). This means that not only will they experience the natural death of their bodies, but their spiritual life will also undergo the death of the soul's separation from God.

The disorder that sin introduces into Adam and Eve's bodily and spiritual lives leads quickly to the disintegration of their relationship to each other. Where they once experienced an original innocence in their sexuality and distinction as man and woman, their sin now introduced a relationship of lust and male domination over women. In the story, Eve explains to God, "I was afraid, because I was naked, so I hid" (Gen. 3:10, NABRE). God goes on to explain the result of her fear by describing the consequences for Adam and Eve's marital relationship: "I will intensify your toil in childbearing; in pain you shall bring forth children. Yet your urge shall be for your husband, and he shall rule over you" (Gen. 3:16, NABRE). To the man, God says, "Cursed is the ground because of you! In toil you shall eat its yield all the days of your life" (Gen. 3:17, NABRE). The meaning of this curse is that from this moment on, man and woman will experience the fruit of their marital union — the blessing of children — in sorrow, pain, and economic hardship. This third curse plays out in many ways today. We can observe all the challenges to family life that originate in the breakdown of the marital relationship — the mistreatment of spouses and children; divorce; economic struggle and every manner of sexual exploitation and abuse; and sins such as adultery, pornography, and sex trafficking. Shame replaced the communion of man and woman's love as husband and wife.

The final curse of Original Sin affects Adam and Eve's relationship to the rest of creation. Their stewardship of the earth turned into exploitation and opposition, as creation became resistant to their dominion, which in time would become oppressive. God says to Adam, "Thorns and thistles [the earth] shall bear for you, and you shall eat the grass of the field. By the sweat of your brow you shall eat bread, until you return to the ground, from which you were taken; For you are dust, and to dust you shall return" (Gen. 3:18–19, NABRE). In other words, humankind would toil for its existence on mere bread and then die. The text contrasts human toil to the leisure of Adam and Eve's dominion over creation, as described in Gen. 1:28–29. Today, more than ever, we see this consequence of Original Sin at work as the human race increasingly exploits the earth and does harm to the environment. The greatest sign of this particular curse, however, is the widespread disease, poverty, migration, and even starvation we continue to experience around the world. These problems are not an accident of nature but are the direct result of human ignorance and selfishness.

Struggling with a fallen nature

These consequences or "curses," as Scripture calls them, have left the human race in a fallen state of Original Sin (CCC 400). Adam and Eve were unable to pass on to their offspring what they had lost by their sin, leaving their descendants without the grace God had originally gifted to the human family. The *Catechism* explains, "All men are implicated in Adam's sin, as St. Paul affirms: 'By one man's disobedience many (that is, all men) were made sinners': 'sin came into the world through one man and death through sin, and so death spread to all men because all men sinned.' The Apostle contrasts the universality of sin and death with the universality of salvation in Christ. 'Then as one man's trespass led to condemnation for all men, so one man's act of righteousness leads to acquittal and life for all men'" (402). The *Catechism* continues as follows:

The transmission of original sin is a mystery that we cannot fully understand. But we do know by Revelation that Adam had received original holiness and justice not for himself alone, but for all human nature. By yielding to the tempter, Adam and Eve committed a *personal sin*, but this sin affected the *human nature* that they would then transmit *in a fallen state*. (404)

Sadly, having lost the grace of original justice, human beings became creatures not even capable of natural happiness, much less the blessedness of Heaven.

Misery quickly covered the earth. This is what it means when Genesis states that God expelled Adam and Eve from the Garden, making it impossible for them to reach the Tree of Life, which symbolizes the source of their happiness and their heavenly home (3:23). God exiled humankind from Paradise to live on the earth by means of our own impoverished resources. The remainder of Genesis tells the story of how human sinfulness spread throughout human society and became increasingly grave by means of murder, idolatry, lustful sex, slavery, and war. As the Church teaches,

> What Revelation makes known to us is confirmed by our own experience. For when man looks into his own heart he finds that he is drawn towards what is wrong and sunk in many evils which cannot come from his good creator. Often refusing to acknowledge God as his source, man has also upset the relationship that should link him to his last end, and at the same time he has broken the right order that should reign within himself as well as between himself and other men and all creatures. (CCC 401)

The Church distinguishes between *Original Sin* and the *personal sins* we commit by our own free choices. All of us inherit Original Sin when our mother conceives us in her womb.

However, it is easier to understand Original Sin not as something we "have" but rather as the absence of the grace of original justice, which God intended for us to have from the beginning. An important principle of life governs this tragedy of our original parents' moral failure: namely, one cannot give what he does not have. By losing the grace of original justice, Adam and Eve were unable to pass this grace on to their offspring. The nature our first parents passed on was a fallen and wounded nature. "It is a sin which will be transmitted by propagation to all mankind, that is, by the transmission of a human nature deprived of original holiness and justice. And that is why original sin is called 'sin' only in an analogical sense: it is a sin 'contracted' and not 'committed'—a state and not an act" (CCC 404). The result is that we remain under the dominion of Satan to a certain extent. "Original sin entails 'captivity under the power of him who thenceforth had the power of death, that is, the devil'" (CCC 407).

The most challenging part of our experience of Original Sin is that sin weakens human nature in numerous ways. For example, sin darkens the mind to the truth and weakens the will, so that we submit to temptation. The appetites of the body can dominate our choices and afflict the soul with urgings and angst. Personal relationships experience strain and misunderstanding, while we also undergo the sufferings of illness, physical degeneration, and finally, death. We also experience a three-fold perversion within our hearts, which the Church calls *concupiscence* (see 1 John 2:16). We call the first perversion the pride of life, which refers to our almost total insistence on being in control of our lives, without reference to God or his law. This represents an idolatry of power. The second is the lust of the eye, by which we tend to envy others and covet what belongs to them, and even wish evil upon them because of their blessings and gifts. The third is the lust of the flesh, by which we desire to satisfy our bodily urges excessively, to the point of violating God's commandments.

These desires rule over us as individuals and as a society. We easily turn things such as food, wealth, drink, and sex into absolute goods of personal gratification, even if doing so deprives others of their happiness and well-being. As the *Catechism* further explains,

> [Original sin] is a deprivation of original holiness and justice, but human nature has not been totally corrupted: it is wounded in the natural powers proper to it, subject to ignorance, suffering and the dominion of death, and inclined to sin—an inclination to evil that is called "concupiscence." Baptism, by imparting the life of Christ's grace, erases original sin and turns a man back towards God, but the consequences for nature, weakened and inclined to evil, persist in man and summon him to spiritual battle. (405)

The greatest challenge of our age, perhaps, is that while we are fully aware of the struggles we face throughout the world, we are under the delusion that we can overcome these difficulties solely by means of knowledge and technique—i.e., by human effort alone.

In the perpetuation of our pride, modern society believes that through research and science, we will be able to conquer the problem of evil. While true knowledge and good practice can help alleviate and even offset some of the effects of Original Sin, according to the Christian perspective, the remedy to the problem of evil must also include faith in God. Faith is the surest way the human person can overcome sin. We do not overcome the effects of Original Sin in this life, but by the grace of baptismal faith, we can bear its curses with hope of final deliverance. Original Sin represents a tremendous struggle in this life, making our earthly existence a constant uphill battle.

As Christians have professed and demonstrated since the beginning, while human effort is important, redemption is not something we are capable of providing for ourselves. Again, we cannot give what we do not possess. This is why we believe that faith in Jesus Christ is so critical. Only God can deliver humanity from the bondage to sin and restore us to the life of grace. Only if a person perseveres in virtue and attains Heaven will she possess a life by which the human person experiences the complete freedom of the children of God, the restoration of integrity, and the glorification of human nature.

God foretold this remedy for sin in Genesis 3:15. The *Catechism* explains, "After his fall, man was not abandoned by God. On the contrary, God calls him and in a mysterious way heralds the coming victory over evil and his restoration from his fall. This passage in Genesis is called the *Protoevangelium* ('first gospel'): the first announcement of the Messiah and Redeemer, of a battle between the serpent and the Woman, and of the final victory of a descendant of hers" (410). In the next chapter, we will look more deeply at the problem of evil and our difficulty in overcoming it.

13

The Problem of Evil

According to Christian revelation, Original Sin has become the legacy of the human race. It has given rise to the problem of evil in the world. Despite our best human efforts, we continue to struggle with many forms of human weakness that inflict harm and misery in our homes, in our communities, and throughout the world. Unlike other animals, human beings are creatures beset with a self-imposed misery. We experience tremendous suffering because of how we act toward God; ourselves; each other; and, more recently, toward the entire planet. We suffer, too, from natural disasters, various infirmities, and endless afflictions. Original Sin has introduced into the created order a deep and profound disorder.

Regardless of our religious convictions, we cannot deny that something is seriously wrong with war and violence, the abuse of children, marital infidelity, lying and cheating, sexual licentiousness, slavery, exploitation and marginalization of the poor, terrorism, substance abuse, pollution, and a whole host of other problems. We also cannot explain these horrible things away or give them a natural explanation. Why do we do these things, and even more, why do we suffer from so many perils, infirmities, and afflictions? In faith, Christians call the problem of evil the "mystery of iniquity." We call it a mystery because the pervasiveness of evil and the perversion of the human heart, generation after generation, are difficult to understand. We seem to know better, but cannot seem to do what we ought (Rom. 7:17–35).

What is evil?

The Church divides evil into two basic categories: physical evil and moral evil. *Physical evils* are those bad things that occur that seem to have no direct correlation to a human choice. For example, we experience physical evil when an earthquake strikes or a tornado levels a town, when a person is born with a serious disfigurement or disability, or when a person suffers from disease or dies unexpectedly. Death itself seems unnatural, even though everyone experiences it. These evils represent forms of suffering that we believe, deep down, ought not to occur. We call these events in life *tragedies*, because we know that something is terribly wrong and out of sorts. While physical evil is not necessarily the direct result of a personal choice, divine revelation indicates that the sin of our first parents is responsible for the disorder the world has experienced ever since: "Following St. Paul, the Church has always taught that the overwhelming misery which oppresses men and their inclination towards evil and death cannot be understood apart from their connection with Adam's sin" (CCC 403).

The reality of *moral evil*, the universal failure to live according to divine wisdom—through the voluntary transgression of the moral law—creates the conditions by which the human person experiences individual failure, personal dysfunction, and social degeneration. This universal disorder of the human heart is a mystery to us in that we do not fully comprehend why our personal choices can be so perverse. Yet the *Catechism* makes it clear that human sin is a fact of human existence. "Sin is present in human history; any attempt to ignore it or to give this dark reality other names would be futile. To try to understand what sin is, one must first recognize *the profound relation of man to God*" (386).

The Church teaches that the first sin entailed Adam and Eve's placing of their own wills before God's plan. The choice to eat from the Tree of the Knowledge of Good and Evil was Adam and Eve's choice to put themselves in the place of God by deciding, for themselves, what was good and evil (CCC 396–398). The first sin was thus a sin of disobedience, which is nothing more than an expression of the inordinate desire for power and control over our lives. Another way to understand the first sin, however, is to recognize the choice "to eat the forbidden fruit" as the choice to covet from God that which we can receive only from God, as his gift. Our life, our flourishing, and our happiness are—and can only ever be—the result of God's gift to us. We do not actually have the power to make ourselves happy. To know this about ourselves, strangely enough, is what it means to have the "knowledge of good and evil."

From the perspective of faith, the life we possess is *not* something we give to ourselves. It is something we receive as a gift from the hand of our Creator—a gift we must receive with gratitude and humility and in obedience to God's love. The irony of the forbidden tree is that when we grasp for what is actually a gift, we show our blindness to what is good and evil. Yet when we receive God's gift of life and love with humility and gratitude, we actually see clearly the difference between good and evil. This is what makes saints holy: they are humble and open to receiving the gift of God's love in their lives. To covet or grasp for the gifts of God, as though we "own" them, is the root of pride. The act of pride is the original form of idolatry, which, Scripture tells us, is a persistent problem in human history. Idolatry did not begin as the worshiping of statues, the earth, the sun, or even other human beings. It began as the sin of a grasping ego, which makes the individual self the source of its own personal fulfillment. One of the reasons God's revelation in Scripture is so valuable, therefore, is that it gives us perspective on the problems of sin, evil, and suffering.

The recurring sin of idolatry

Most of salvation history up to the coming of Christ unfolds over roughly two thousand years. Adam and Eve were deceived by the devil's temptation, as we know — thus resulting in a terrible moral blindness that increasingly made humankind ignorant of the truth of God's love and his ways. Humanity became confused about who and what God is and began to worship other things. As idolatry spread, ancient peoples became increasingly ignorant of God's plan (the divine economy) and fell into greater pride and division. This is the meaning of the story of the Tower of Babel (Gen. 11:1–9). As the Church explains, "This state of division into many nations is at once cosmic, social and religious. It is intended to limit the pride of fallen humanity united only in its perverse ambition to forge its own unity as at Babel. But, because of sin, both polytheism and the idolatry of the nation and of its rulers constantly threaten this provisional economy [of salvation] with the perversion of paganism" (CCC 57).

In the Old Testament, the book of Wisdom states, "But wretched are they, and in dead things are their hopes, who termed gods things made by human hands: Gold and silver, the product of art, and images of beasts, or useless stone, the work of an ancient hand" (13:10, NABRE). Even worse, Scripture tells us that the worship of these idols was actually a veiled worship of demons. Satan managed to subject the human race to himself by deceiving humanity into worshiping objects far beneath the dignity of the human person. Instead of having *dominion* over creation, the devil tricked humanity into *worshiping* creation. This is why St. Paul exhorts the Corinthians, who had converted from idol worship, as follows: "Therefore, my beloved, shun the worship of idols. I speak as to sensible men; judge for yourselves what I say.... I imply that what pagans sacrifice they offer to demons and not to God. I do not want you to be partners with demons" (1 Cor. 10:14, 20).

The further humanity fell into these sins, the worse idolatry became, and vice versa. One of the most horrific expressions of demonic worship came in the form of human sacrifice, and even the sacrifice of innocent children. Human beings attained the pinnacle of this fallen state when entire civilizations began to worship other sinful human beings as gods, such as when the ancient Egyptians worshiped Pharaoh. This is the worst form of idolatry — to worship as God a perverse and sinful man who requires human sacrifice. We see something similar at work today with the idolatry of sex — idolatry that leads to abortion. One of the consequences of making sexual freedom an absolute value is the total disregard for the life of the unborn. As Scripture makes abundantly clear, even God's own people Israel struggled to overcome the sin of idolatry: "They sacrificed their sons and their daughters to the demons; they poured out innocent blood, the blood of their sons and daughters, whom they sacrificed to the idols of Canaan; and the land was polluted with blood" (Ps. 106:37–38).

In the Letter to the Romans, St. Paul states that those who fell into idolatry, especially his own people, "have no excuse; for although they knew God they did not accord him glory as God or give him thanks. Instead, they became vain in their reasoning, and their senseless minds were darkened" (1:20–21, NABRE). St. Paul continues by recounting the gradual descent of humanity into the gravest of sins. What is important is how God responds to our persistent desires to have our own way. God's response to this is to allow us to suffer by our own self-imposed moral depravity: "Therefore, God handed them over to impurity through the lusts of their hearts for the mutual degradation of their bodies ... And since they did not see fit to acknowledge God, God handed them over to their undiscerning mind to do what is improper. They are filled with every form of wickedness, evil, greed, and malice; full of envy, murder, rivalry, treachery, and spite" (Rom. 1:24, 28–29, NABRE). How much more true all of this is for people today, even now that Christ has come into the world and the Church has spent two thousand years proclaiming the gospel. As we consider God's response to human sin, we see that He never wills suffering or evil of any kind, but he does allow it. He has a reason for this, which we will consider later.

The sad irony in the pattern of human sinfulness is that when the human person loses touch with the true God, he loses himself in the process. Idolatry leads to a lost sense of human dignity. In order to remember our dignity, we must recover the true worship of God. Christians believe that we know ourselves truly as God's beloved children only when we are in relationship with our Father. We see this dynamic at work in the world even today. The more people lose the sense of God, the more sin abounds. The more sin abounds, the more people lose their connection to God and to one another. Through new forms of idolatry, many people today have abandoned the worship of God and thus have placed their faith in creatures and in the work of their own hands. We see people devoting themselves religiously to things such as making money, sexual activity, health and exercise, and entertainment. Not that these are bad things in themselves, but we often give to them an importance they do not have. The Church calls these modern tendencies toward idolatry *neo-paganism*.

When we look around the world, many people are also openly embracing lifestyles that are contrary to God's plan for human happiness. People's hearts have become hardened to those ways that lead to human flourishing. The more these sins are embraced, the more miserable people become, leading them to descend deeper into lives of suffering. What looks like freedom and happiness at first becomes enslavement to the darkening of the mind and the tyranny of fleshly desires and addictions. One might be tempted to ask, "Where is God in all this misery? Does he care about us?" The answer we receive in the Bible is a definitive yes! God does care, and he is *always* present to us and desires to save us from our self-imposed misery.

God's plan of redemption and the problem of suffering

So where is God in all of this misery? The "handing over" that St. Paul described as God's "wrath" is the key to understanding how God responds to human pride. We might think of God as a raging and abusive parent, but the biblical notion of God's wrath reveals God to be like a father patiently waiting out his son's folly — think of the father in the parable of the prodigal son (Luke 15:11–32). God's punishment for sin — the first step of his plan to redeem us — is always to allow us to experience and live with the consequences of our own free choices, only to lose our freedom to multiple forms of enslavement in the end. Only then is the human person able to come to his senses, as did the prodigal son, and recognize the need to return to God.

For many today, the realities of evil and suffering present occasions to doubt God's existence, or at least to doubt that God really cares about us. Often, when people become agnostic or atheistic, it is because they have experienced a tragedy in their lives for which they have no explanation. They feel abandoned by God and unfairly punished by life, and thus withdraw into themselves as they search for other ways to ease the pain and despair that come with experiencing sin and evil. This can lead people to blame God for evil and to reject him, even to deny his existence completely. If God is all-loving and all-good, then why would he allow people to suffer, especially innocent people and children, most of all? It seems unfair that God would allow this to happen if he could do something about it.

While many people today do not like the word *sin*, we call moral evil *sinful* because morally evil acts are offenses against God's generosity, human dignity, and the universal desire for peace. Sin is a rejection of true love. What makes it even worse is that we are unable to do anything about sin by our own efforts. Despite our best intentions to make things better, we have very little success. History is a stark reminder that moral evil is part of our personal experience. As the *Catechism* puts it, "Without the knowledge Revelation gives of God we cannot recognize sin clearly and are tempted to explain it as merely a developmental flaw, a psychological weakness, a mistake, or the necessary consequence of an inadequate social structure, etc. Only in the knowledge of God's plan for man can we grasp that sin is an abuse of the freedom that God gives to created persons so that they are capable of loving him and loving one another" (387).

While it is awful to experience evil and suffering, we can grasp why God permits these experiences, if we keep two things in mind. First, as we learn from Scripture, the abuse of freedom is what brings evil into the world. God does not cause evil. We do. To see the connection between freedom and sin is critical. God allows evil to occur and to spread because he respects and honors freedom. He knows that without freedom, there is no love. The communion of love we have spoken about previously would be impossible without freedom. Yet with the freedom of a finite creature, there is also the possibility of failure. Angelic and human persons are capable of choosing wrongly and acting in ways that harm their relationships with God, themselves, each other, and the rest of creation.

Thus, God always respects our freedom, and he will never force himself upon an unwilling soul. Notice St. Paul's appeal to the

Galatians: "Formerly, when you did not know God, you were in bondage to beings that by nature are no gods; but now that you have come to know God, or rather to be known by God, how can you turn back again to the weak and beggarly elemental spirits, whose slaves you want to be once more?" (Gal. 4:8–9). St. Paul goes on to appeal to their conscience: "For you were called to freedom, brethren; only do not use your freedom as an opportunity for the flesh" (Gal. 5:13). The deepest meaning of the Fall of Adam and Eve is that the abuse of freedom has real consequences, not just for individuals but also for the entire community of God's creation.

The second thing to keep in mind is that no creature exists as an isolated individual. Each is part of an integral and interdependent order of being—a community of creatures that flourish only within the context of those interdependent relationships. This community is the image of the trinitarian God. However, this also means that when members of that community sin, they harm the entire society of God's creation. Think of creation like a spiderweb. When one strand of the web is touched, the entire web moves. Break a few of the essential strands of the web, and the entire thing collapses. This is a good analogy for how creation exists as a community of beings. The angels and the human race exist within creation as those essential strands that hold the entire web of created existence together. This is why St. Paul says,

> For creation awaits with eager expectation the revelation of the children of God; for creation was made subject to futility, not of its own accord but because of the one who subjected it, in hope that creation itself would be set free from slavery to corruption and share in the glorious freedom of the children of God. We know that all creation is groaning in labor pains even until now; and not only that, but we ourselves, who have the firstfruits of the Spirit, we also groan

within ourselves as we wait for adoption, the redemption of our bodies. (Rom. 8:19–23, NABRE)

While it might seem unfair that sin affects the whole of creation, that one member suffers because of the sins of another member, that is nevertheless the nature of personal communion. Love cannot exist without these interrelationships of dependency and self-gift. To offend those relationships by sin is bound to undermine the communion of love and do it tremendous harm. God's plan to create a community of being ran the risk of the suffering that might come from the vulnerabilities of such interdependence. Yet in God's mind, the risk of love is always worth it. God's only other option was to create nothing whatsoever.

Because of the problems of both Original Sin and personal sin, Christians believe that humanity is in need of God's salvation and redemption. Only God can deliver us from our misery. The good news is that God's love and goodness are greater than any sin his creatures could commit. In other words, God cannot eliminate the possibility of suffering and evil without eliminating freedom and the possibility of love. However, because God is all-powerful, he can bring a greater good out of any evil we might produce. There is no evil God's love cannot conquer. What Christians believe with a firm hope is that "after his fall, man was not abandoned by God. On the contrary, God calls him and in a mysterious way heralds the coming victory over evil and his restoration from his fall" (CCC 410). We will look in the next chapter at God's plan of salvation, which culminates in the coming of Jesus Christ.

14

Jesus the Messiah

The previous two chapters have shown the story of human history as a bleak tale of ignorance and sin. The moral degeneration that followed the Fall is not the entire story, however. In fact, it serves rather as a backdrop to a much more important story: the story of God's unfolding plan to redeem the human race from all that prevents us from realizing the fullness of God's purpose for our lives. To conquer the problem of evil is not a simple, easy, or straightforward endeavor, as though God can simply snap his fingers and make it all disappear. The process of redemption is just that—a process. It takes time and involves a gradual transformation and maturation of the human race. This is true of the entire human family as a whole and of each person. Sanctification from sin is a developmental process of growth requiring the free cooperation of the human person. While we cannot save ourselves on our own, God does not save us without our cooperation.

This explains why God uses covenants as the primary way through which to unfold his plan of salvation (see CCC 54–67). A covenant is a unique kind of relationship that God establishes with us. At the heart of a covenant is an oath of fidelity. God swears an oath and pledges a complete gift to us of his love. Those with whom God enters into covenants also swear an oath of fidelity to God. The essence of this covenant relationship is familial. By entering into covenants with different people and, eventually, with the entire human family, he establishes a familial bond with the human race. Think of a marriage — the reason spouses take vows is that they are forming a familial, covenantal bond with each other. They are doing this to pledge their love to each other and to promise to each other the entire gift of their lives — that they might become one family together. In the ancient world, people often created family ties by making covenants with other tribes.

God's covenantal love for humanity

We already looked briefly at the covenant line recounted in Scripture. Let us take a closer look now to see how God's plan of redemption unfolded. In Scripture, the first covenant God makes is with Adam and Eve. While the first covenant is not so explicitly stated, we can see it in the first chapter of Genesis when God looks upon everything he has made and declares it to be "very good" (1:31). Then, on the seventh day, God rests from all his work. In Scripture, the number seven actually means "covenant." Throughout Scripture, God re-creates that seventh day; that is, he makes covenants with different people. In all, God made six covenants with the human race. After the Fall of Adam and Eve, God promises that he will save the human race by sending a Redeemer who will defeat the power of evil in the world (Gen. 3:15). As we saw before, the Church calls this promise the *protoevangelium*, which simply means the "first gospel." The prophecy foreshadows the coming of a son of Eve who will crush the head of the serpent. God fulfilled this promise of redemption gradually through the unfolding covenant relationship he originally made with the human family through Adam and Eve.

After the covenant with Adam and Eve, the covenant line passed to their son Abel, who made an acceptable sacrifice to God (Gen. 4:8–16). However, Abel's brother Cain killed him out of jealousy. The covenant line then passed through Adam and Eve's third son Seth to Noah, who delivered his family and the animals from the Great Flood. God made a new covenant with Noah and his descendants. The covenant God made with Noah included the entire human family and remained until the coming of Christ. Eventually, however, due to humanity's persistent clinging to idolatry, God singled out one family line through whom he would fulfill his plan. Thus, the covenant line passed through Noah's son Shem and, eventually, down to Abraham (see Gen. 5–9 for the account of the Flood and the story of Noah's sons).

God made the third covenant with Abraham. Abraham is called the *father of faith*, and he became the father of many nations through his obedience to God's promises. The *Catechism* says, "The people descended from Abraham would be the trustees of the promise made to the patriarchs, the chosen people, called to prepare for that day when God would gather all his children into the unity of the Church" (60). Abraham bears a special honor as the patriarch of faith because, amidst the widespread practices of idolatry and iniquity during his time, Abraham heard God call to him. Abraham rejected idolatry and faithfully obeyed God, even to the point of offering his own son Isaac as a sacrifice to God. God did not make Abraham follow through with the sacrifice of Isaac, but he did use this moment to prophesy that one day, he himself would offer his own Son as the sacrifice to end all sacrifices, an eternal offering that would atone for all human sin (Gen. 22:1–18).

It is to Abraham that God promised what today we call the Holy Land. He also promised that Abraham's name would be great and his descendants many. In short, God promised to Abraham through faith what all the surrounding nations acquired by conquest — a great name, many descendants, and wealth. Today, people might think God did not treat Abraham well, especially in asking him to sacrifice Isaac. It can also seem strange that God would promise Abraham worldly blessings, such as a great name and wealth. However, we have to keep in mind that God had to establish his relationship with ancient peoples in a language and manner they could understand. We call this way of doing things *divine accommodation*. God often gets our attention by accommodating himself to our moral understanding and thereby leading us to a deeper understanding of his will. This is what God did with Abraham.

Abraham was the patriarch of three subsequent covenant patriarchs — Isaac, Jacob, and Joseph. Through Abraham's bloodline, the covenant line thus passed eventually to Moses, who led the Israelite people out of slavery in Egypt, bringing them back to the land Abraham had inherited from God. The *Catechism* states, "After the patriarchs, God formed Israel as his people by freeing them from slavery in Egypt. He established with them the covenant of Mount Sinai and, through Moses, gave them his law so that they would recognize him and serve him as the one living and true God, the provident Father and just judge, so that they would look for the promised Savior" (62). God made the fourth covenant, then, with the Israelite people under the leadership of Moses. Sadly, the problem of idolatry remained a consistent problem for the Israelites from this time on.

Once resettled in the Promised Land, the Israelite people became a great kingdom under David, with whom God made the fifth covenant. God promised to David that the Messiah would be born of his lineage (2 Samuel 7:13–16). The Gospels call Jesus the son of David for this reason. Not long after David died, however, the Israelites fell into idolatry (again), being influenced more by the surrounding nations than by any remembrance of their covenant with God. Eventually, God had to exile his fallen people to a foreign land, where they finally learned that there is only one God and that he alone is to be adored, loved, and worshiped (read 1 and 2 Kings for an account of the rise and fall of the kingdom).

During this time of exile and suffering, God sent the prophets to encourage his people to believe that he was with them and would eventually save them from their exile and, more importantly, from the curse of sin and death: "Through the prophets, God forms his people in the hope of salvation, in the expectation of a new and everlasting Covenant intended for all, to be written on their hearts. The prophets proclaim a radical redemption of the People of God, purification from all their infidelities, a salvation which will include all the nations" (CCC 64). During the time of the prophets, God began to foretell explicitly the coming of the Messiah — the one whom God would send, and the one who would be both son of man and Son of God. God also promised that he himself would come among us to save us and lead us as our King (Jer. 32:37–41).[9]

All the covenants God made in the Old Testament possessed both a tremendous promise of hope and an inherent weakness. The promise of hope was that God would be faithful to the covenant, even if we had been unfaithful. The inherent weakness of the covenants was that they depended on human faithfulness. In particular, they relied upon the Law of Moses and the human capacity to follow that law, a capacity that was practically nonexistent. Despite their very best efforts, the People of God could not avoid falling into idolatry and the sins of their neighbors.

---

[9] For a wonderful and detailed account of salvation history, see John Bergsma's book *Bible Basics for Catholics: A New Picture of Salvation History* (Notre Dame, IN: Ave Maria Press, 2015).

What is perplexing, however, is that God promised by the power of his Word that his people would be faithful to the covenant. He made this promise repeatedly. For example, the prophet Jeremiah says,

> See, days are coming ... when I will make a new covenant with the house of Israel and the house of Judah. It will not be like the covenant I made with their ancestors the day I took them by the hand to lead them out of the land of Egypt. They broke my covenant, though I was their master ... But this is the covenant I will make with the house of Israel after those days ... I will place my law within them, and write it upon their hearts; I will be their God, and they shall be my people. They will no longer teach their friends and relatives, "Know the Lord!" Everyone, from least to greatest, shall know me ... for I will forgive their iniquity and no longer remember their sin. (Jer. 31:31–34, NABRE)

God did not merely promise that *he* would be faithful; he promised that *his people* would be faithful as well. Here is another passage, which is just as powerful, from the prophet Ezekiel:

> Then the nations shall know that I am the Lord ... when through you I show my holiness before their very eyes. I will take you away from among the nations, gather you from all the lands, and bring you back to your own soil. I will sprinkle clean water over you to make you clean; from all your impurities and from all your idols I will cleanse you. I will give you a new heart, and a new spirit I will put within you. I will remove the heart of stone from your flesh and give you a heart of flesh. I will put my spirit within you *so that you walk in my statutes, observe my ordinances, and keep them.* (Ezek. 36:23–27, NABRE, emphasis mine)

Yet the entire history recounted in the Old Testament tells us that these covenants failed to establish a permanent bond of fidelity on the part of God's people.

God's faithfulness is beyond our wildest dreams

How, then, did God fulfill the promise that *we* would be faithful, when human weakness prevents this from happening? God fulfills his promise by waiting until his people are truly ready to accept his gift of redemption. This readiness did not come in the form of human perfection, but in the form of human failure. God's people were ready when they finally realized by the end of their exile that they could not fulfill their side of the covenant. They began to cry out for God's salvation. Sadly, this did not occur until the Israelites returned to their land and were made a vassal (slave) kingdom under the empires of the Greeks and the Romans, who attempted to force Israel to become an idolatrous people. (For this history, read First and Second Maccabees.)

The irony of this history and struggle with idolatry is that when the Israelites were free to worship God, they did not. Yet when foreigners *forced* them to worship false gods, the Israelites finally realized their deep desire to worship the God who had, all this time, remained in covenant with them. Yet they were persecuted for doing so. This persecution led to their deep cry for God's deliverance. The same is true for any human being. When we are free to unite ourselves to God, we often insist proudly on our own way. Yet when we find ourselves enslaved by sin, our hearts cry out to God for help. God knows this about us, so it should not surprise us that the whole of human history is a story of how God humbles us to the point of our opening our hearts to him.

God waits until we are ready to receive his grace of redemption. The problems of idolatry and the blindness of sin explain why it takes God time to roll out his plan of salvation. God remains faithful to his covenant. He is faithful to his people and to each of us. We must realize that God knows human willpower cannot deliver the human race from sin and death. He knows we cannot be faithful to the covenant without his assistance. He knows we have to become humble before we can receive his grace—we have to suffer before we desire deliverance. St. Paul thus explains how the Mosaic Law functioned only to instruct us: "Now before faith came, we were confined under the law, kept under restraint until faith should be revealed. So that the law was our custodian until Christ came, that we might be justified by faith. But now that faith has come, we are no longer under a custodian" (Gal. 3:23–25). God gave the law so that Israel might, in humility, become receptive to the grace of God given upon the coming of the Messiah. The same is true for the entire human family. Israel's story is thus our story.

The time of the Old Testament, therefore, was a period of preparation for the grace God would give the entire world through Jesus Christ. St. Paul sums up the first five stages of salvation history as follows:

> I mean that the heir, as long as he is a child, is no better than a slave, though he is the owner of all the estate; but he is under guardians and trustees until the date set by the father. So with us; when we were children, we were slaves to the elemental spirits of the universe. But when the time had fully come, God sent forth his Son, born of woman, born under the law, to redeem those who were under the law, so that we might receive adoption as sons. (Gal. 4:1–5)

We can grasp the beauty of God's plan, however, only when we see how God fulfilled his promise that *we* would be faithful to the covenant. The prophet Ezekiel hints at how God would accomplish this great work:

No longer shall they defile themselves with their idols, their abominations, and all their transgressions. I will deliver them from all their apostasy through which they sinned. *I will cleanse them so that they will be my people, and I will be their God. David my servant shall be king over them; they shall all have one shepherd. They shall walk in my ordinances, observe my statutes, and keep them.* They shall live on the land I gave to Jacob my servant, the land where their ancestors lived; they shall live on it always, they, their children, and their children's children, with David my servant as their prince forever. I will make a covenant of peace with them; it shall be an everlasting covenant with them. I will multiply them and put my sanctuary among them forever. My dwelling shall be with them; I will be their God, and they will be my people. Then the nations shall know that I, the Lord, make Israel holy, by putting my sanctuary among them forever. (Ezek. 37:23–28, NABRE)

This passage is so important that I would ask you to read it through several times. The rest of what I will present in this book is truly about how God fulfills this prophecy.

To understand that God will be faithful is not difficult—he is God. Nevertheless, how would he render *us* capable of being faithful to the covenant? It was not by force or by magic. It was by sending his Son into the world as a human being. It was through the Incarnation of God's Word in the Person of Jesus Christ that God fulfilled his promise (see CCC 461–470). In a sense, God *did* make us capable of being faithful. Yet he did not do this by taking away our freedom. God destroyed the power of human sinfulness by assuming a human nature and redeeming the human family from within. He did not merely declare our salvation or cover up our iniquity. He actually redeemed human nature by his Incarnation, through uniting his divine nature to human nature and, thus, providing a way by which grace could transform every human person. God did this without in any way negating the importance of human freedom. The *Catechism* thus states that God became man for these reasons: to reconcile us to himself, to make known his love for us, to be a model of holiness for us, and to make us partakers in his divine nature (457–460).

The key is to understand that the God-Man Jesus Christ used his freedom to place himself into a perfect union with God the Father, to restore the covenantal communion God established in the beginning with Adam and Eve. St. Paul calls Jesus the *Second* or *Last Adam* (1 Cor. 15:45–47). The Church Fathers call Jesus the *New Adam*. His obedience and faithfulness won for the rest of us the grace of salvation and union with God forever. Yet God maintained the necessity of our freedom. Within the wisdom of God's plan is an essential dimension of justice. Just as it is unjust for us to disregard God's love and law, so too would it be unjust for God to save humanity by negating human freedom and forcing us into a false reconciliation with him. We must freely embrace God's love, and yet without the grace of God, we are unable to do this adequately. To restore us to union with God, Jesus had to exercise his freedom to offer himself and human nature to the Father in love. By this self-gift, Jesus restored to the human race, for all time, access to the Holy Spirit, by which we can freely receive God's love and give ourselves to God in return.

The New Covenant

This great exchange of love is what we celebrate in the suffering, death, resurrection, and ascension of Jesus. What the Church calls the *Paschal Mystery* is the great event that fully enacts the redemption of the human race and restores human nature to communion

with God (CCC 595–667). It is through the Paschal Mystery that
God established the sixth covenant with the human family, which
we call the *New Covenant*. By his Passion, Jesus gave himself entirely to the Father on our behalf. He offered our human nature in
love to God in return for all the gifts God has given us. The most
beautiful part is that Jesus made this offering while shouldering
the entire curse of Adam's sin. That is, not by superpowers did he
save us, but precisely by entering fully into the depths of human
misery and suffering — i.e., the entire legacy of human sin — and
then offering that suffering in love to the Father.

The prophet Isaiah described this event hundreds of years
before Jesus came to earth. The suffering servant song in Isaiah
52–53 captures the essence of how Jesus redeemed humanity by
bearing the curse of sin as a "an offering for sin" (53:10). St. Paul
explains, "For our sake he made him to be sin who knew no sin, so
that in him we might become the righteousness of God" (2 Cor.
5:21). The suffering servant song is a long passage, but it captures
the essence of what Jesus has done for humanity by bearing the
curse of Adam:

> It was our pain that he bore, our sufferings he endured. We
> thought of him as stricken, struck down by God and afflicted,
> but he was pierced for our sins, crushed for our iniquity. He
> bore the punishment that makes us whole; by his wounds we
> were healed. We had all gone astray like sheep, all following
> our own way; but the Lord laid upon him the guilt of us all.
> Though harshly treated, he submitted and did not open his
> mouth; like a lamb led to slaughter or a sheep silent before
> shearers, he did not open his mouth. Seized and condemned,
> he was taken away. Who would have thought any more of his
> destiny? For he was cut off from the land of the living, struck
> for the sins of his people. He was given a grave among the

wicked, a burial place with evildoers, though he had done no wrong, nor was deceit found in his mouth. But it was the Lord's will to crush him with pain. By making his life as a reparation offering, he shall see his offspring, shall lengthen his days, and the Lord's will shall be accomplished through him. Because of his anguish he shall see the light; because of his knowledge he shall be content; my servant, the just one, shall justify the many, their iniquity he shall bear. Therefore I will give him his portion among the many, and he shall divide the spoils with the mighty, because he surrendered himself to death, was counted among the transgressors, bore the sins of many, and interceded for the transgressors. (Isa. 53:4–12, NABRE)

Thus, through Jesus' Passion, suffering and misery — what Satan initiated and what remains because of original and personal sin — can become for any believer an acceptable offering of perfect love to our Heavenly Father. The crucifix is thus, for Christians, the symbol of God's self-offering to redeem us, and our self-offering to him in return.

During the Easter Vigil, the Church proclaims, "Oh happy fault [of Adam] that earned for us so great, so glorious a Redeemer!" This prayer is deeply mysterious, because it essentially states that God has taken what is so depraved — suffering and death — and transformed it by his love into a perfect offering. In Christ, the suffering that comes from sin has become the path of redemption and renewal for all those who put their faith in Jesus Christ. Belief is essential here, because we must believe that God has done this for us in Jesus and that through faith, we unite ourselves to Jesus' eternal offering of love to the Father. His sacrifice becomes the path by which we can return to our Father's house, just as the prodigal son did. If we do not believe this, then it can have no effect in our lives. Without trust in the love of another, there can be no true relationship of love and communion. Yet faith is difficult, which is why grace comes to us as internal support to our natural freedom.

15

The Holy Spirit and the Mystical Life

To believe that God has done so much for humanity in Jesus Christ is also to believe that we truly have access to the Father through the Son in the power of the Holy Spirit. The question is how this works. How is it possible to have access to the Father, even now in this time, if Jesus no longer walks the earth? In the first place, we must keep in mind that Christianity is not a "religion of the book" or a mere philosophy of good living—a moral code we attempt to imitate. While Christians do have a sacred text that exhorts us to live well, the primary contribution Christianity makes to the human race is the gift of the Holy Spirit, which communicates the very life of God and eradicates the problem of evil from the human heart.

The New Covenant is effective precisely because of the presence of the Holy Spirit. Quoting the prophet Joel, St. Peter declares on the Jewish feast day of Pentecost, when the Holy Spirit descended upon the Church, "And in the last days it shall be, God declares, that I will pour out my spirit upon all flesh, and your sons and your daughters shall prophesy, your young men shall see visions, your old men shall dream dreams" (Acts 2:17). This Jewish feast day commemorated the giving of the Mosaic Law at Mount Sinai. On the Christian feast of Pentecost, the Church celebrates the day when God replaced the law written on stone with a new law written on the hearts of all humankind—hearts made of flesh, full of the love of the Holy Spirit, as Joel foretold.

The gift of the Holy Spirit

Jesus has left us with a means by which he gives to us everything his Word proclaims and the power by which we can actually live authentic and holy human lives. The gift of the Holy Spirit enables a person to be faithful to God's covenant, as promised in the Old Testament: "I will put my spirit within you, and cause you to walk in my statutes and be careful to observe my ordinances" (Ezek. 36:27). With the Spirit of God dwelling within the soul, one can be faithful to God, just as God is faithful to us. This is how God fulfills his promise that *we* will be faithful. This is what Christians mean when they speak about the grace of God. Grace is the gift of the Holy Spirit. The New Covenant in Christ is the full realization of God's plan for salvation. This blessed life of grace culminates in the resurrection of our bodies at the end of history.

One might ask, how do we receive the Holy Spirit today, two thousand years after Pentecost? The Church teaches that we receive the grace (or gift) of the Holy Spirit through the seven great signs (sacraments) of the Church: baptism, confirmation, the Eucharist, reconciliation, holy orders, holy matrimony, and the anointing of the sick. As the *Catechism* explains, "The purpose of the sacraments is to sanctify men, to build up the Body of Christ and, finally, to give worship to God. Because they are signs they also instruct. They not only presuppose faith, but by words and objects they also nourish, strengthen, and express it" (1123). Jesus continually gives the Holy Spirit through the liturgical and sacramental life of His Church, which is his Body.

The three primary sacraments that establish a person in the life of the Holy Spirit are baptism, confirmation, and the Eucharist.

By *baptism*, the Holy Spirit regenerates and makes the baptized person a child of God. By *confirmation*, the Holy Spirit gives the baptized person the ability to live as a disciple of Jesus Christ in the world, even in the face of suffering, evil, and even persecution. Through the *Eucharist*, which is truly the Body and Blood of Jesus, the Holy Spirit nurtures the spiritual life for growth by giving us the risen Christ to consume as food. Jesus says this explicitly in the Gospel of John:

> Amen, amen, I say to you, unless you eat the flesh of the Son of Man and drink his blood, you do not have life within you. Whoever eats my flesh and drinks my blood has eternal life, and I will raise him on the last day. For my flesh is true food, and my blood is true drink. Whoever eats my flesh and drinks my blood remains in me and I in him. Just as the living Father sent me and I have life because of the Father, so also the one who feeds on me will have life because of me. (6:53–57, NABRE)

The Eucharist works within each person to build up the Church in the unity of love, in order to carry out the mission of Jesus Christ in the world. The Eucharist is thus the source of the Church's growth, as well as the realization of the communion of love God has always intended for and proposed to the human family by means of his covenants.

If you recall from a previous chapter, the Holy Spirit is the third Person of the Trinity. He exists as the love shared by the Father and the Son. He *is* the love of the Father and the Son. When we receive the Holy Spirit at baptism, God re-creates us in grace and unites himself to us through the dwelling of the Spirit within our souls. Besides forgiving all sin, the presence of the Spirit fills the soul with spiritual gifts, including the virtues of faith, hope, and charity. The Spirit plants within the soul the seeds of every moral virtue — prudence, justice, temperance, and fortitude — and empowers us to live faithfully by giving us the seven gifts named in Isaiah: "The spirit of the Lord shall rest upon him, the spirit of wisdom and understanding, the spirit of counsel and might, the spirit of knowledge and the fear of the Lord. And his delight shall be in the fear of the Lord" (11:2–3).

Through the gift of grace, as the Spirit, God Himself comes to dwell in us in person. Thus, Christianity is a religion of personal relationship and friendship with God. This is how St. Paul explains it: "Therefore, since we are justified by faith, we have peace with God through our Lord Jesus Christ. Through him we have obtained access [by faith] to this grace in which we stand, and we rejoice in our hope of sharing the glory of God.... Because God's love has been poured into our hearts through the Holy Spirit who has been given to us" (Rom. 5:1–2, 5). Christianity is thus far more than an ideal moral code or some distant aspiration of personal perfection. It satisfies the deepest longings of the heart, because it gives us what we most deeply desire — divine love and communion with God.

Life in the Spirit

The Christian life is a life *in* the Holy Spirit and an existence endowed with divine life from our Heavenly Father. By the power and presence of the Holy Spirit dwelling within our souls, God makes us partakers of his divine nature, thus fulfilling all of his covenant promises. As we saw before, and it is worth repeating, St. Peter explains it like this: "His divine power has bestowed on us everything that makes for life and devotion, through the knowledge of him who called us by his own glory and power. Through these, he has bestowed on us the precious and very great promises, so that through them you may come to share in the divine nature, after escaping from the corruption that is in the world because of evil desire" (2 Pet. 1:3–4, NABRE). Concisely, by the gift of the Spirit, the Father makes a person a child of God, not just in name but also in reality. That is, a baptized person is God's very own offspring. Together, the baptized become God's covenant family, which we call *the Church*.

Throughout the ages, as we have seen, God has been forming a covenant people to call his own and in whom he will fulfill his promises of love and communion. As the Church explains,

> "The eternal Father, in accordance with the utterly gratuitous and mysterious design of his wisdom and goodness, created the whole universe and chose to raise up men to share in his own divine life," to which he calls all men in his Son. "The Father ... determined to call together in a holy Church those who should believe in Christ." This "family of God" is gradually formed and takes shape during the stages of human history, in keeping with the Father's plan.... "Established in this last age of the world and made manifest in the outpouring of the Spirit, it will be brought to glorious completion at the end of time." (CCC 759)

Christians believe that the Church, though still deeply affected by human frailty and sinfulness, is the privileged place where the entire human family has access to Jesus through the Spirit in every age, until he returns at the end of history.

The reason for this belief, as was stated above, is that the principal means by which God gives us supernatural life is through the sacraments of the Church. This is where, under ordinary circumstances, the Holy Spirit shows up. This is not to suggest that the Spirit is not present everywhere. However, the Spirit draws people to the Church, and through the sacramental life of the Church, God unites himself to those who believe. This is why Christians say that the Church is necessary for salvation. To enjoy spiritual union with God by the Holy Spirit is to participate in the reality of the Church—and this is so by God's design. The sacraments are thus the ritual celebrations by which the Church participates in the mystery of God's own life and the work of Christ our Redeemer:

> It is this mystery of Christ that the Church proclaims and celebrates in her liturgy so that the faithful may live from it and bear witness to it in the world: "For it is in the liturgy, especially in the divine sacrifice of the Eucharist, that 'the work of our redemption is accomplished,' and it is through the liturgy especially that the faithful are enabled to express in their lives and manifest to others the mystery of Christ and the real nature of the true Church." (CCC 1068)

Besides the sacraments, and especially within the liturgy, the Holy Spirit is present in the prayerful reading of Scripture as well. "The Holy Spirit gives a spiritual understanding of the Word of God to those who read or hear it, according to the dispositions of their hearts" (CCC 1101). As we saw previously, Scripture is the Church's sacred text that contains the written and inspired memory of God's words and deeds throughout salvation history. The Church compiled the Scriptures, and she relies on them for fidelity to revealed truth and for instructing the faithful in the way of discipleship. As St. Paul explains to Timothy, "All scripture is inspired by God and profitable for teaching, for reproof, for correction, and for training in righteousness, that the man of God may be complete, equipped for every good work" (2 Tim. 3:16–17).

Thus, in a profound way, God communicates his divine life and the many gifts of grace in and through the sacraments of the Church. The liturgy provides the most important context for reading Scripture and understanding it properly. Liturgy is not a mere ritual service or celebration—like a birthday party—that commemorates our Faith or gets us together periodically as an association of people. Rather, liturgy grants us the opportunity to enter into and share in the mystery of God's divine life through an ever-growing union with the Holy Spirit. As the *Catechism* says, "The Spirit and the Church cooperate to manifest Christ and his work of salvation in the liturgy. Primarily in the Eucharist, and by analogy in the other sacraments, the liturgy is the *memorial* of the mystery of salvation. The Holy Spirit is the Church's living memory" (1099). Scripture uses the Greek term *anamnesis* to describe this memorial. This word does not mean a mere recollection of events past; rather, through the power and presence of the Holy Spirit, the liturgy makes the mystery of salvation truly present to each generation of believers.

The Holy Spirit thus dwells within us and through the Church's liturgy, which is the privileged setting for the sacred reading of Scripture. If a person cooperates with the Spirit of God, participation in the life of the Church will inevitably effect growth in holiness:

> The Holy Spirit is "the principle of every vital and truly saving action in each part of the Body [the Church]." He works in many ways to build up the whole Body in charity: by God's Word "which is able to build you up"; by Baptism, through which he forms Christ's Body; by the sacraments, which give growth and healing to Christ's members; by "the grace of the apostles, which holds first place among his gifts"; by the virtues, which make us act according to what is good; finally, by the many special graces (called "charisms"), by which he makes the faithful "fit and ready to undertake various tasks and offices for the renewal and building up of the Church." (CCC 798)

Sacramental grace transforms the inner life gradually so that one bears more and more the likeness of Jesus, who is our brother in nature. Grace transforms the mind in truth, strengthens the will in love, and restores the integrity of the emotional landscape of the human heart. In short, participating in the full life of the Church, including all her sacraments, heals the faithful disciple of the effects of original and personal sin and restores one's nature to wholeness.

Sanctification through the Church

We call this process of healing and sanctification the *spiritual* or *mystical* life. According to what Christ has established, it is impossible to live fully the spiritual life unless the disciple belongs to and participates in the full life of the Church. "In the Church this communion of men with God, in the 'love [that] never ends,' is the purpose which governs everything in her that is a sacramental means, tied to this passing world" (CCC 773). There is no such thing as a private Faith, an individualistic spirituality, or a solitary Christian. Christian discipleship is not a matter of mere human striving toward excellence. While the Christian life is a struggle—a cross to bear—only together, united in the Body of Christ, do Jesus' disciples receive the full measure and outpouring of God's Spirit. Only when one receives as a gift all that Christ has instituted for human salvation is one able to grow fully in the union of love the Father desires.

The reason Jesus established the Church and instituted the sacraments, therefore, is that the sanctification of the human heart in love is not instantaneous. To return to a concept we have dealt with previously, God always honors human freedom. Freedom is the minimum requirement of love. Thus, the Church and her sacraments are always present to us, but one must respond to the call of the Holy Spirit and receive from the Spirit the inspiration to participate in the spiritual (mystical) life of Christ's Body. Jesus describes it like this: "As the Father loves me, so have I loved you;

abide in my love. If you keep my commandments, you will abide in my love, just as I have kept my Father's commandments and abide in his love. These things I have spoken to you, that my joy may be in you, and your joy may be full" (John 15:9–11). To remain in Christ's love requires that we freely obey all of Jesus' commands, including those pertaining to the moral law and the full participation in the life of the Church.

Again, God never forces his love upon us, nor does he simply brush sin to the side. Rather, he invites us to hear his Word, extends the invitation of his grace, and then draws us to himself within the community of faith through the gentle and interior movement of the Spirit that transforms the heart. "By the working of grace the Holy Spirit educates us in spiritual freedom in order to make us free collaborators in his work in the Church and in the world" (CCC 1742). The action of the Spirit is not a force that pushes from behind, but an invitation that moves one inwardly to respond to the gift of God's love. This is similar to how beauty elicits love in the heart. The draw to beauty constitutes both the external presence of the other and the inward movement of love for the other.

Love is how the power of the Spirit affects a person. It moves the soul toward God, as desire moves the heart to what is beautiful. St. Paul explains in his Letter to the Romans, "'The word is near you, in your mouth and in your heart' ... for, if you confess with your mouth that Jesus is Lord and believe in your heart that God raised him from the dead, you will be saved. For one believes with the heart and so is justified, and one confesses with the mouth and so is saved" (10:8, 9–10, NABRE). It should be obvious that no one can "believe in the heart" or "confess with the lips" if coerced to believe or if violated in the name of God. The requirement of freedom and the gentleness of the Spirit explain why an authentic and humble proclamation of the gospel (and not its imposition) is so vital to Christian evangelization. The Word proclaimed is a word of love addressed to the human heart. When a disciple of Jesus gives witness to the love of God in his life, the other who hears him encounters the Word as a call, and can experience an awakening within the heart of spiritual hunger for God's love. It should thus be evident that any attempt by Christians to force the Faith on another is an offense against the Holy Spirit and the spiritual life.

Membership in the Church guarantees that any baptized person has access to the redeeming love of Christ. The power of the Holy Spirit present within the Church—the one who is the love of the Father and the Son—is what guarantees our access to grace. It is not that God's grace cannot operate outside the Church, for it surely can, but we can be certain that the grace we need is available to us if we remain within the Church. To be a member of the Church, however, does not *guarantee* a person's faithfulness to God's covenant—as if sanctification is automatic. By participation in the Body of Christ, a person has access to the grace of God, and yet human freedom is still operative. One still has to allow Christ to redeem the inner self freely through the power of the Holy Spirit. If one perseveres in living the spiritual life until death, her soul will attain eternal union with God in the Beatific Vision of Heaven. In the next chapter, I will consider the nature of the Church and describe how we know which Church Christ established.

16

The Church of Jesus Christ

If full participation in the life of the Church is so crucial to the spiritual life and to having access to the Holy Spirit, how is a person to know whether he or she belongs to the Church that Christ established? In the course of history, many Christian associations have claimed to be the true Church of Christ. From the earliest centuries of the Church, Christians have believed that the true Church of Christ professed the entire revelation of God. Any group that introduced a gospel other than that preached by the apostles was not of the sheepfold of Christ. As St. Paul reminds the Church in Corinth,

> For I am jealous of you with the jealousy of God, since I betrothed you to one husband to present you as a chaste virgin to Christ. But I am afraid that, as the serpent deceived Eve by his cunning, your thoughts may be corrupted from a sincere [and pure] commitment to Christ. For if someone comes and preaches another Jesus than the one we preached, or if you receive a different spirit from the one you received or a different gospel from the one you accepted, you put up with it well enough ... For such people are false apostles, deceitful workers, who masquerade as apostles of Christ. And no wonder, for even Satan masquerades as an angel of

light. So it is not strange that his ministers also masquerade as ministers of righteousness. Their end will correspond to their deeds. (2 Cor. 11:2–4, 13–15, NABRE).

In a similar but even more forceful manner, Paul chastises the Galatians, "I am amazed that you are so quickly forsaking the one who called you by [the] grace [of Christ] for a different gospel (not that there is another). But there are some who are disturbing you and wish to pervert the gospel of Christ. But even if we or an angel from heaven should preach [to you] a gospel other than the one that we preached to you, let that one be accursed!" (Gal. 1:6–8, NABRE).

The formulation of creeds was an essential development of Christ's Church and an indispensable expression of the Faith as it developed within the earliest Christian communities. Within the first century or so, the Church began to develop formal summaries of the true Faith to protect the faithful against false teachings. The word *creed* comes from the Latin *credo*, which means "I believe." We also use the word *credimus*, which means "we believe." In the earliest formulations, these were the first words of the Creed: "I (we) believe in one God, the Father Almighty, Creator of heaven and earth."

The rule of faith

In the ancient Church, the Fathers called the Creed a "symbol" of the Faith. This term comes from the Greek word *symbolon*, which "meant half of a broken object ... The broken parts were placed together to verify the bearer's identity. The symbol of faith, then, is a sign of recognition and communion between believers" (CCC 188). Simply stated, a creed is a brief summary of the essential core beliefs of Christianity, especially those beliefs about God that distinguish Christianity from all the other religions of the world. Early on, the community of disciples professed its faith in these short statements, which the community used to distinguish true disciples from those who were spreading erroneous ideas about the Faith. In this way, one could identify the true Church Christ founded by whether or not a particular community of disciples had preserved every element of the apostolic teaching.

Over the centuries, the Church has adopted a number of different creeds. In each case, the Faith remained the same, but depending upon the needs of a given time, the Church used a creedal statement to elaborate or clarify certain doctrines of the Faith for the faithful. This includes those teachings that pertain to the Church herself. In the most ancient creedal formulas, the faithful professed the Church to be one, holy, catholic, and apostolic. I will unpack the meaning of these "marks" of the Church in a moment. The most recent creed is Pope St. Paul VI's *Solemni hac liturgia* (Credo of the People of God), which he promulgated in 1968. This creed is lengthier and explains the Faith in more detail for modern peoples.

Not only is preserving and handing on the Faith important to the leaders of the Church, but all Christians of the ancient world were eager to profess (or declare) their faith in the God of Jesus Christ before others. This might explain why the early Church was persecuted and blessed with so many martyrs. A disciple is not able to spread the gospel if she is unwilling to share her faith with others — to be a witness. While the Faith belongs first to the Church, because the Church has many members, each member must also profess his faith before others. Christians can do this in many ways, the most important way being to share their stories of God with others — that is, telling the stories of what God has done in their day-to-day lives. St. Paul does so before his fellow Jews when he recounts to them his conversion story: "As I drew near to Damascus, about noon a great light from the sky suddenly shone around me. I fell to the ground and heard a voice saying to me, 'Saul, Saul, why are you persecuting me?' I replied, 'Who are you, sir?' And he said to me, 'I am Jesus the Nazorean whom you are persecuting.' My companions saw the light but did not hear the voice of the one who spoke to me" (Acts 22:6–9, NABRE). We also witness by doing works of mercy to others in the name of Jesus.

Creeds help us profess our faith publicly by summarizing for us the essential tenets of Christian belief. Thus, we have to distinguish between *personal* faith and *private* faith. The Christian Faith is deeply personal, because each believer must profess freely his faith in Jesus from the heart. The Christian Faith, however, is not private, because disciples of Jesus do not make up what they believe according to their own personal preferences. Nor do they keep the Faith to themselves. The content of the Faith precedes any individual's personal coming to faith. By the assent of faith, a person is received into the Faith of the Church. This is why a new adult convert to Christianity recites the Creed before receiving the sacrament of baptism. When the Church baptizes a baby, the parents do this on their child's behalf. Thus, the Church ties the Creed closely to the sacrament of baptism. The Church baptizes a new Christian (neophyte) *into* the Faith of the Church.

The practice of professing the Faith in summary form goes all the way back to the apostles themselves. St. Paul, for example, provides several summaries of the Faith in his apostolic letters. In one of the more famous summaries, he states,

> For I delivered to you as of first importance what I also received, that Christ died for our sins in accordance with the scriptures, that he was buried, that he was raised on the third day in accordance with the scriptures, and that he appeared to

Cephas, then to the twelve. Then he appeared to more than five hundred brethren at one time, most of whom are still alive, though some have fallen asleep. Then he appeared to James, then to all the apostles. Last of all, as to one untimely born, he appeared also to me. (1 Cor. 15:3–8)

One of the earliest Church Fathers, St. Cyril of Jerusalem, was a bishop renowned for his writings on the sacrament of baptism and the process by which new converts became members of the Church. He wrote this about the earliest creedal formulas: "This synthesis of faith was not made to accord with human opinions, but rather what was of the greatest importance was gathered from all the Scriptures, to present the one teaching of the faith in its entirety. And just as the mustard seed contains a great number of branches in a tiny grain, so too this summary of faith encompassed in a few words the whole knowledge of the true religion contained in the Old and the New Testaments" (quoted in CCC 186).

The first and perhaps earliest "official" creed is the *Apostles' Creed*. We call it that because we believe the original formulation of this creed dates back to the apostles. What we know from the Apostles' Creed is that the Church summarized her belief in the Holy Trinity very early on. This creed is divided up into twelve statements, called *articles*, one for each of the apostles. While it took several centuries for the earliest creeds to take their final form, the Church framed these symbols of the Faith to resolve certain theological disputes that arose in the Church and to ensure unity of belief about the God of Jesus Christ.

The creed with which Catholics are most familiar is the *Niceno-Constantinopolitan Creed,* or simply the *Nicene Creed*. Catholics most commonly recite this creed each Sunday at Mass. It, too, has twelve articles, but it elaborates on certain points more than the Apostles' Creed does. The reason for this is that in the early

The Catholic Faith Explained

Church, different beliefs about Jesus Christ began to spread that were contrary to Apostolic Tradition. For example, some Christians began to spread the idea that Jesus was not God. Others argued that Jesus was God, but not also a human being. Others believed that Jesus was neither God nor man but some other deity. In order to ensure that the faithful would retain a true understanding of Jesus Christ — that he is fully God and fully man through the Incarnation of the Word — the Church developed the earlier creeds into a more elaborate profession of faith. Take a few minutes to read the Apostles' and Nicene Creeds and note the differences and similarities between them.

Apostles' Creed

I believe in God,
the Father almighty,
Creator of heaven and earth,

and in Jesus Christ, his only Son, our Lord,
who was conceived by the Holy Spirit,
born of the Virgin Mary,
suffered under Pontius Pilate,
was crucified, died and was buried;
he descended into hell;
on the third day he rose again from the dead;
he ascended into heaven,
and is seated at the right hand of God the Father almighty;
from there he will come to judge the living and the dead.

I believe in the Holy Spirit,
the holy catholic Church,
the communion of saints,
the forgiveness of sins,
the resurrection of the body,
and life everlasting. Amen.

The Church of Jesus Christ

Nicene Creed

I believe in one God,
the Father almighty,
maker of heaven and earth,
of all things visible and invisible.

I believe in one Lord Jesus Christ,
the Only Begotten Son of God,
born of the Father before all ages.
God from God, Light from Light,
true God from true God, begotten, not made, consubstantial with the Father; through him all things were made.
For us men and for our salvation he came down from
heaven, and by the Holy Spirit was incarnate of the Virgin Mary, and became man. For our sake he was crucified
under Pontius Pilate, he suffered death and was buried,
and rose again on the third day in accordance with the
Scriptures. He ascended into heaven and is seated at the
right hand of the Father. He will come again in glory to
judge the living and the dead and his kingdom will have
no end.

I believe in the Holy Spirit, the Lord, the giver of life, who
proceeds from the Father and the Son, who with the Father
and the Son is adored and glorified, who has spoken through
the prophets. I believe in one, holy, catholic and apostolic
Church. I confess one Baptism for the forgiveness of sins and
I look forward to the resurrection of the dead and the life of
the world to come. Amen.

Both creeds contain twelve articles of faith, but probably more
evident is the fact that the Church divides each creed into three
parts.

The first part speaks about the Father, the Creator of Heaven and earth. We profess that the Father is the source of the entire Godhead—the Almighty One. As we saw previously, Jesus refers to the Father on many occasions in the Gospels. The second part of the Creed professes the Christian faith in Jesus Christ. Christian belief about Jesus is probably the most difficult part of the Nicene Creed to understand. The Creed explains that Jesus is fully God and fully human at the same time. By reflecting on many different passages from Scripture, the Church Fathers used different philosophical concepts to help explain the mystery of Jesus' divine sonship. The Nicene Creed is thus echoing the words of St. Thomas the Apostle, who, upon placing his finger in the wounds of the risen (and human) body of Jesus declared in faith, "My Lord and my God!" (John 20:28).

The third part of the Creed addresses the third Person of the Trinity, the Holy Spirit, and his relationship with the Church; the forgiveness of sins; and the resurrection of the body at the end of time. In this third part, the Church professes her faith in the nature of the Body of Christ and its essential constitution. Therein, the Creed states that the Church is one, holy, catholic, and apostolic. Christians identified these four marks in the first creeds professed in the liturgy of the ancient Church. The true Church Christ founded, therefore, will always profess the Creed at the liturgy and safeguard these four characteristic marks of the community of faith. I would like to end this chapter by reflecting on what each of these marks of the Church means.

The marks of the Church Christ founded

The *oneness* of the Church is rooted in the presence of the Holy Spirit, who unites Christians as one Body in Christ. In his Letter to the Ephesians, St. Paul exhorts the members of the Church to cultivate this unity: "I ... urge you to live in a manner worthy of the call you have received, with all humility and gentleness, with patience, bearing with one another through love, *striving to preserve the unity of the spirit* through the bond of peace: one body and one Spirit, as you were also called to the one hope of your call; one Lord, one faith, one baptism; one God and Father of all, who is over all and through all and in all" (4:1–6, NABRE, emphasis mine). Clearly, Scripture reveals there is to be one Church. From the beginning, the Spirit has moved Christians to expand the one Church to the ends of the earth. However, Christians were not to splinter off and start autonomous churches. The mission for which Christ came to redeem humanity is to establish the one Kingdom of God on earth. I will further address the unity of the Church in the next chapter.

The Church is *holy* because of the presence of the Holy Spirit and because, despite the sins of her members, the Church is the Body of Christ. As the *Catechism* explains, "This is because Christ, the Son of God, who with the Father and the Spirit is hailed as 'alone holy,' loved the Church as his Bride, giving himself up for her so as to sanctify her; he joined her to himself as his body and endowed her with the gift of the Holy Spirit for the glory of God" (823). Does this mean there is no sin among the Church's members? No, of course not! Christians can often be unfaithful to God because, again, God does not impose his love upon human beings, even his disciples. Christians are always free to reject the grace of the Holy Spirit. Thus, the Church exists for sinners, and she is comprised of sinners. As the *Catechism* further expounds, "'The Church on earth is endowed already with a sanctity that is real though imperfect.' In her members perfect holiness is something yet to be acquired: 'Strengthened by so many and such great means of salvation, all the faithful, whatever their condition or state—though each in his own way—are called by the Lord to that perfection of sanctity by which the Father himself is perfect'" (825).

Most adult Christians belong to the Church not because they are perfect but because they seek the holiness of life only the Spirit can give. Of course, as the apostle Judas demonstrates, Jesus associates even with betrayers who can cause tremendous scandal. Nevertheless, the lack of holiness in the Church's members should never be a reason to start a new church, to go out on one's own, or to abandon the Faith altogether. The zealous ideal of a "church without sinners" has always been a cause of division within the Body of Christ, and never the cause of her unity and holiness. An old adage can help the faithful avoid discouragement in the face of gross human failure: a disciple ought never to abandon Jesus because of Peter's denial, and a disciple ought never to abandon Peter because of Judas's betrayal.

Moving to the third mark, the Church is *catholic* because she is a communion of love intended for all peoples, without distinction. The word *catholic* literally means "universal." As St. Paul writes to the Galatians, "For in Christ Jesus you are all sons of God, through faith. For as many of you as were baptized into Christ have put on Christ. There is neither Jew nor Greek; there is neither slave nor free; there is neither male nor female; for you are all one in Christ Jesus. And if you are Christ's, then you are Abraham's offspring, heirs according to promise" (3:26–29). This catholicity also means that "Christ is present in her ... In her subsists the fullness of Christ's body united with its head; this implies that she receives from him 'the fullness of the means of salvation' which he has willed: correct and complete confession of faith, full sacramental life, and ordained ministry in apostolic succession" (CCC 830).

Not only is the Church catholic because she transcends individual and local identities, but also because she retains *all* the means by which Christ has sanctified the human race. The Catholic

Church calls herself "the" and not "a" church because, historically, she has maintained all that Christ instituted for the salvation of humanity. The historical problem of some Christian groups is that they have put their ethnic or national identity first, or they have separated themselves—sometimes unknowingly—from some of the means of sanctification, such as the full sacramental life or the entire teaching of Scripture; or they have rejected the governing structures of the Church that Christ established. These historical divisions represent a deep wound in the heart of Jesus and require the great effort of every Christian to overcome. Jesus desires unity among his followers, as we have seen already.

Finally, the Church is *apostolic*, because Jesus founded her upon the Faith of the twelve apostles who accompanied him during his earthly life:

> The Church is apostolic because she is founded on the apostles, in three ways: she was and remains built on "the foundation of the Apostles," the witnesses chosen and sent on mission by Christ himself; with the help of the Spirit dwelling in her, the Church keeps and hands on the teaching, the "good deposit," the salutary words she has heard from the apostles; she continues to be taught, sanctified, and guided by the apostles until Christ's return, through their successors in pastoral office: the college of bishops, "assisted by priests, in union with the successor of Peter, the Church's supreme pastor." (CCC 857)

The true Church of Christ must therefore profess the same Faith that the apostles did.

The Church is apostolic for another reason as well. Every Christian must go out and bring the gospel to every person (1 Cor. 9:16). The word *apostle* means "one who is sent." The apostolic nature of the Church requires Christians to go out and proclaim the gospel to all people. Christians do not believe that the Faith is a private matter to be kept to ourselves. As the *Catechism* explains, "The Lord's missionary mandate is ultimately grounded in the eternal love of the Most Holy Trinity: 'The Church on earth is by her nature missionary since, according to the plan of the Father, she has as her origin the mission of the Son and the Holy Spirit.' The ultimate purpose of mission is none other than to make men share in the communion between the Father and the Son in their Spirit of love" (850).

Jesus calls every disciple to own the mission of salvation—to make disciples of all nations (Matt. 28:19). As we have seen already, there are good and bad ways to do this. The work of evangelization is not compatible with any attempt to pressure, coerce, or mandate faith in the name of Jesus Christ. This is why the Church believes that the proper response to religious and cultural diversity is always respectful dialogue and a commitment to peaceful coexistence: "The *right to the exercise of freedom*, especially in moral and religious matters, is an inalienable requirement of the dignity of the human person" (CCC 1738).

The Holy Spirit guarantees these four marks of the Church as a pledge of God's covenantal fidelity on behalf of the redemption of the human family. While the Catholic Church remains united to the successor of Peter in Rome (that is, the pope), she extends far beyond the church in Rome, comprising twenty-four different liturgical rites across the globe. A common misunderstanding is that the Catholic Church includes only the Roman Church. Rather, she includes any Christian community that has remained in communion with the Bishop of Rome. This communion is not a mere sentiment among Christians, but tied indefectibly to the established structures of the Church and her governance. As the *Catechism* summarizes,

> Fully incorporated into the society of the Church are those who, possessing the Spirit of Christ, accept all the means

of salvation given to the Church together with her entire organization, and who—by the bonds constituted by the profession of faith, the sacraments, ecclesiastical government, and communion—are joined in the visible structure of the Church of Christ, who rules her through the Supreme Pontiff and the bishops. Even though incorporated into the Church, one who does not however persevere in charity is not saved. He remains indeed in the bosom of the Church, but "in body" not "in heart." (CCC 837)

Regardless of what the members of the Church do from a purely human (and even sinful) point of view, the Father ensures that he will fulfill his covenant promises in and through his Son's Church. He ensures that those who believe in Jesus Christ can be faithful to the covenant, that is, so long as they participate fully in the life of the one, holy, catholic, and apostolic Church. The Church thus insists that "all men are called to this catholic unity of the People of God.... And to it, in different ways, belong or are ordered: the Catholic faithful, others who believe in Christ, and finally all mankind, called by God's grace to salvation" (CCC 836).

17

A Living Tradition

One might ask how the Catholic Church has remained, through-out the ages, true to the four marks of the Church. The Catholic Church is the oldest uninterrupted institution in history, which itself is a miracle and evidence of the Spirit's presence within the Church. Keep in mind that the covenants previously recounted happened a very long time ago. Divine revelation is, in one sense, a long-past event, even while it also remains a living reality in the life of the Church. The historical continuity of the Church is not an accident or the consequence of luck, though. During the course of his earthly ministry, Jesus established the Kingdom of God — the community of his followers as the new Israel, or People of God. He established this Kingdom as an everlasting one.

The promise made to David

The first thing Jesus did was to give the Church a basic structure by which the community would remain unified and be able to carry out the mission he gave them — to preach the gospel to the ends of the earth (Acts 1:1–9). That basic structure consisted of the twelve apostles, whom Jesus ordained as "overseers," or the first bishops, of the Church and to whom he gave the authority (in his name) to do three things: (1) proclaim the gospel, (2) share the grace of the Holy Spirit, and (3) govern the Church. He gave a unique and singular role to Peter, the leader of the apostles, to fulfill this three-fold mandate. If Jesus is the king of God's Kingdom, Peter is the Kingdom's prime minister or steward. This is the meaning of Jesus' giving Peter the "keys" to the Kingdom (Matt. 16:19).

This conferral of authority was prefigured in the Davidic Kingdom of the Old Testament (Isa. 22:22). As we saw previously with Ezekiel's prophecy, the last covenant God would establish would be the restoration of the Davidic Kingdom. This would be an everlasting covenant: "David my servant shall be king over them; and they shall all have one shepherd … and David my servant shall be their prince forever. I will make a covenant of peace with them; it shall be an everlasting covenant with them" (Ezek. 37:24, 25–26). The Church is that Kingdom, and Jesus is God's eternal servant, David, since Jesus is both the Son of God and the son of David (Luke 1:32). The Kingdom Jesus established on Peter's confession of faith that he is "the Christ, the Son of the living God" was prefigured by a prophecy made to King David himself when he was still alive: "The Lord will make you a house. When your days are fulfilled and you lie down with your fathers, I will raise up your offspring after you, who shall come forth from your body, and I will establish his kingdom. He shall build a house for my name, and I will establish the throne of his kingdom forever. I will be his father, and he shall be my son" (Matt. 16:16; 2 Sam. 7:11–14).

The promise God made through his covenants was not merely to send Jesus to die for our sins and then rise from the dead, but for Jesus to establish the Kingdom of God on earth, as a real kingdom with its own governing structure, laws, and resources — just as God had established a kingdom in Israel under David (Matt. 3:2). The difference would be that Jesus would not tie his kingdom to any particular piece of real estate. Rather, it would exist as a universal communion of believers, joined in the Spirit. During his trial, Jesus declared, "My kingdom does not belong to this world. If my kingdom did belong to this world, my attendants [would] be fighting to keep me from being handed over to the Jews. But as it is, my kingdom is not here" (John 18:36, NABRE). What he meant was that the Kingdom of God is no earthly kingdom.

Powerfully, nearly three hundred years before the coming of Jesus, the Old Testament prophet Daniel foretold the establishment of the Church. While interpreting a dream for the Babylonian king Nebuchadnezzar, Daniel explains,

> O king, you saw a statue, very large and exceedingly bright, terrifying in appearance as it stood before you ... While you watched, a stone was hewn from a mountain without a hand being put to it, and it struck [the statue's] iron and clay feet, breaking them in pieces. The iron, clay, bronze, silver, and gold [of the statue] all crumbled at once, fine as the chaff on the threshing floor in summer, and the wind blew them away without leaving a trace. But the stone that struck the statue became a great mountain and filled the whole earth. (Dan. 2:31, 34–35, NABRE)

Daniel goes on to interpret the meaning of the dream as follows: "In the lifetime of those kings the God of heaven will set up a kingdom that shall never be destroyed or delivered up to another people; rather, it shall break in pieces all these kingdoms and put an end to them, and it shall stand forever" (Dan. 2:44, NABRE). For Catholics, Daniel's prophecy explains the significance of Jesus' changing Simon's name to *Peter*, which means "the rock." The Church established on Peter's profession of faith is the Kingdom that God established in Christ (Matt. 16:15–20).

The Catholic Faith Explained

A universal and worldwide kingdom

By establishing God's Kingdom on earth, Jesus would bring his ministry of redemption successfully to the entire human race through the proclamation of the gospel (Acts 1:6–8). The revelation of God needed not only to be remembered but also to be shared with all people until the end of time, as Jesus commanded his apostles to do. Two thousand years have passed, and the Church has successfully transmitted the revelation of God — the gospel of Jesus Christ — to the entire planet. The Church exists on every continent and within every nation of the world. So how has the Church succeeded in doing this?

As we saw when we discussed the feast of Pentecost, God sent the Holy Spirit to empower the Church to accomplish the mission of proclaiming the gospel (Acts 2:1–13). In the power of the Spirit, the apostles went out into the world to establish new local communities of believers, who, in turn, went out and proclaimed the gospel to others. As the *Catechism* states,

> Christ the Lord, in whom the entire Revelation of the most high God is summed up, commanded the apostles to preach the Gospel, which had been promised beforehand by the prophets [*such as Daniel and Isaiah*], and which he fulfilled in his own person and promulgated with his own lips. In preaching the Gospel, they were to communicate the gifts of God to all men. This Gospel was to be the source of all saving truth and moral discipline. (75, emphasis mine)

In the beginning, Jesus' disciples were all Jews sent out to other Jews to share the incredible news that Jesus had risen from the dead and was their long-awaited Messiah. By the power of the Holy Spirit, many Jewish people came to believe in Jesus (Acts 2:41). However, it did not take long before non-Jewish people, or Gentiles, began to believe in Jesus also and receive the Holy Spirit

(Acts 10:34–48). The Christian Faith thus grew rapidly, because the apostles preached the saving message of Jesus Christ.

In the beginning, the Church had no written testimonies of the life of Jesus or of encounters with him—these would come later. The faithful simply preached the gospel and taught others what they had learned and experienced about Jesus while he was on earth. They also shared with great enthusiasm the transforming effects Jesus had had on their personal lives. As they preached, they performed miracles and brought healing, just as Jesus did. Thus, the Holy Spirit gave the apostles the same power that Jesus had exercised (Acts 3:1–10). An important aspect of the preaching of the apostles is how they demonstrated, by the deep conviction of their proclamation, that all the promises of the Old Testament had finally been fulfilled in Jesus (Acts 2:14–36; 3:11–26; 7). Even more, the promise of salvation was continuing in the life and ministry of the Church, as the gospel message spread throughout the region we know presently as the Holy Land.

The other important work the apostles accomplished, as they spread out to establish new communities of the one Church, was to celebrate the liturgy. Most importantly, the Church commemorated the Last Supper by celebrating what, today, the Church calls the *Mass* or *Divine Liturgy*. That is, from the beginning, the first Christians celebrated the Lord's Supper—the *Eucharist*, which means "thanksgiving." They also healed people, baptizing and confirming them through the laying on of hands. They also ordained more and more men as bishops, priests, and deacons, so that the Church could continue to grow. Eventually, as the geographic expanse of the Church enlarged, the apostles began to teach through writing letters, mostly to encourage new believers how to grow in their newfound faith in Jesus Christ. St. Paul's letters have become the most instructive to us. Paul was originally a scholar of the Jewish law, before he encountered Christ, and he was instrumental in founding many new communities among the Gentiles throughout the Roman Empire. He had a particular gift for explaining the Christian Faith, and we might even call him the Church's first theologian. Thankfully, the Holy Spirit also inspired the apostles, along with certain of their companions, to record their memories of Jesus' life and teachings. These writings are the four Gospels of Matthew, Mark, Luke, and John. The Gospels are the primary accounts of Jesus' life and teachings to this day.

The three pillars of the Christian Faith

As the community of Christians grew and matured, and as the Faith was handed on to more and more people, the Church established three pillars that would preserve and safeguard the revelation of God. These three pillars are Apostolic (or Sacred) Tradition, Sacred Scripture, and the Magisterium (or teaching office) of the Church. The interdependency of these three pillars has helped the Church preserve divine revelation and spread the Christian Faith, in perfect continuity and without error, all the way up to the present moment. Think of these pillars as the three legs of a stool. All three legs are necessary for the stool's stability. The truths of our Faith are preserved and handed on precisely because the Church has depended upon all three equally. Let us look at each one of these pillars now to understand how each has contributed to the handing on of the Christian Faith.

As we have seen already, the apostles and their successors established Sacred Tradition by their preaching, both in speech and in writing, as well as by their actions. The *Catechism* explains, "In keeping with the Lord's command, the Gospel was handed on ... 'by the apostles ... by the spoken word of their preaching, by the example they gave, by the institutions they established, what they themselves had received—whether from the lips of Christ, from his way of life and his works, or whether they had learned it at the prompting of the Holy Spirit'" (76). As the *Catechism* goes on to explain, "This living transmission, accomplished in the Holy Spirit, is called Tradition, since it is distinct from Sacred Scripture, though closely connected to it. Through Tradition, 'the Church, in her doctrine, life and worship, perpetuates and transmits to every generation all that she herself is, all that she believes'" (78). Tradition has remained a living source of the Church's Faith down through the ages, through the succession of bishops as well as through the Church's celebration of the liturgy. We have also come to rely upon the "sayings of the holy Fathers [later bishops]," who were also "[witnesses] to the life-giving presence of this Tradition, showing how its riches are poured out in the practice and life of the Church, in her belief and her prayer" (CCC 78).

When we speak about Tradition, however, we are not speaking about customs or conventions the Church has adopted over the centuries, which reflect not so much the Eternal Word of God but the cultural practices and habits of the various peoples who have accepted the Christian Faith throughout the ages. "Tradition is to be distinguished from the various theological, disciplinary, liturgical or devotional traditions, born in the local churches over time. These are the particular forms, adapted to different places and times, in which the great Tradition is expressed. In the light of Tradition, these traditions can be retained, modified or even abandoned under the guidance of the Church's Magisterium" (CCC 83). Precisely through accommodating local customs in this way, the Church respects local cultures, while also preserving the universal character of the Faith. What we see within the Catholic (universal) Church, then, is diversity within unity — a perfect image of the Trinity.

The second pillar by which the Church has transmitted the gospel is Sacred Scripture. The Bible is comprised of seventy-three different books (*bible* literally means "books") that tell the story of salvation history from Adam until the death of the last apostle, John, who died of old age on the island of Patmos in the Mediterranean Sea. The writings in Scripture span centuries, but they tell one continuous story of God's saving plan to redeem humanity, as we have seen already. The Old Testament has forty-six books, while the New Testament contains twenty-seven. The People of God (Jewish and Christian) assembled each testament according to different types of writings, and both testaments follow the same basic structure.

The Old Testament begins with the Law (the Torah), followed by the historical books, such as 1 and 2 Kings. The wisdom literature, including the Psalms and Proverbs, follows the historical books, and the Old Testament ends with a collection of prophetic writings, such as those of Isaiah and Ezekiel. The New Testament begins with the New Law, contained in the four Gospels (Matthew, Mark, Luke, and John). The Gospels are followed by the Acts of the Apostles, which is an early Church history. After this, we have a collection of apostolic letters, which convey Christian wisdom, and then the entire Bible ends with the book of Revelation (literally, "apocalypse"), which presents a mysterious prophetic vision about the end times and Christ's return.

While the Church completed the sacred writings of the New Testament within seventy years of Jesus' death, she did not finalize the list of sacred writings until the fourth century after Christ. The Greek translation of the Scriptures, which ancient Christians read at Eucharist, contained the books that most Jews read during the first century. This is why the Church decided that these books would comprise the official collection we call *Sacred Scripture*. Protestant communities have fewer books in their version of the Old Testament, because the protestant reformers adopted a Jewish (not Greek) version of the Old Testament that Jewish leaders codified years after Jesus died. The Catholic Church, however, has always used the older Greek collection of Old Testament writings, which the Jewish people used during the time of Jesus.

How the Faith gets handed down through the ages

We believe the Bible is the *inspired* Word of God: "To compose the sacred books, God chose certain men who, all the while he employed them in this task, made full use of their own faculties and powers so that, though he acted in them and by them, it was as true authors that they consigned to writing whatever he wanted written, and no more" (CCC 106). Thus, God is the primary author of Scripture, while the human authors offered their own unique writing abilities and perspectives, which they shared through the grace of their personal faith. Scripture is thus inspired because "the divinely revealed realities, which are contained and presented in the text of Sacred Scripture, have been written down under the inspiration of the Holy Spirit" (CCC 105). When we say the Spirit inspired the human authors, we do not mean that the Spirit moved them emotionally, although this might have happened, but that the Spirit enlightened and influenced them to write what they wrote—by giving them not a dictation, but an inner comprehension of the truths God desired to have written down.

The Church also believes that Scripture is *inerrant,* or without error: "Since therefore all that the inspired authors or sacred writers affirm should be regarded as affirmed by the Holy Spirit, we must acknowledge that the books of Scripture firmly, faithfully, and without error teach that truth which God, for the sake of our salvation, wished to see confided to the Sacred Scriptures" (CCC 107). Those truths about which Scripture does not err are those truths that pertain to faith and morals. Without these truths, we cannot be redeemed from sin, nor can we reach Heaven. This narrows the scope a bit. God does not mean for us to learn the laws of physics, chemistry, or any other science from Scripture.

As we saw at the beginning of this book, we are to accept the historical truth of the biblical narratives that were intentionally written as historical accounts. We are thus to interpret Scripture by taking into consideration the intentions of the sacred authors. As the *Catechism* explains, "In order to discover *the sacred authors' intention*, the reader must take into account the conditions of their time and culture, the literary genres in use at that time, and the modes of feeling, speaking and narrating then current. 'For the fact is that truth is differently presented and expressed in the various types of historical writing, in prophetical and poetical texts, and in other forms of literary expression'" (110).

Fundamentalism—taking the Scriptures at face value—becomes a problem when we do not follow certain interpretive guidelines. The first such guideline is to avoid taking any passage of Scripture out of context. We must read every passage of God's Word in light of the entire Bible, because the *whole* Word of God helps us grasp *each* word of God. Second, we must always rely upon Apostolic Tradition to guide the reading of Scripture. Sacred Tradition helps us grasp what we are to believe, since Scripture is not a self-interpreting collection of writings. Finally, we will understand Scripture best when we begin to see how all the truths of faith play together like a symphony. The Church sums up the correct approach in this way:

> In Sacred Scripture, God speaks to man in a human way. To interpret Scripture correctly, the reader must be attentive to what the human authors truly wanted to affirm, and to what God wanted to reveal to us by their words.... But since Sacred Scripture is inspired, there is another and no less important principle of correct interpretation, without which Scripture would remain a dead letter. "Sacred Scripture must

be read and interpreted in the light of the same Spirit by whom it was written." (CCC 109, 111)

Because Scripture is not easy to interpret or understand, Christians also believe that God has entrusted the interpretation of his Word to the teaching authority of the Church, which we call the *Magisterium*.

The teaching office of the apostles and their successors, the bishops, is the third leg that supports the handing on of God's Word down to our own time. The Magisterium is comprised of all the bishops in communion with the successor of Peter when they teach as one on any truth pertaining to faith or morals—any truth God has revealed for our salvation in Jesus Christ. The Magisterium does not have authority regarding other areas of truth, such as truths of physics, psychology, or economics, but only those truths that comprise the Faith of the Church as God has revealed them to his People. On matters of Christian faith, Catholics believe that when the Magisterium teaches, it does so consistently, without error.

The *Catechism* explains it like this: "'The task of giving an authentic interpretation of the Word of God, whether in its written form or in the form of Tradition, has been entrusted to the living teaching office of the Church alone. Its authority in this matter is exercised in the name of Jesus Christ.' This means that the task of interpretation has been entrusted to the bishops in communion with the successor of Peter, the Bishop of Rome" (85). The Magisterium, however, "is not superior to the Word of God, but is its servant. It teaches only what has been handed on to it. At the divine command and with the help of the Holy Spirit, it listens to this devotedly, guards it with dedication and expounds it faithfully. All that it proposes for belief as being divinely revealed is drawn from this single deposit of faith" (CCC 86). This exercise of magisterial authority has resulted in a rather large body of teachings and practices, which we call the *Deposit of Faith*. Think of the Deposit of Faith as a storehouse or treasury of sacred truth and practices of discipleship that help the faithful to become and truly remain the holy People of God.

The teaching office of the Church is also expressed in another manner. When Christians are faithful to the whole of God's Word, as it has been passed down, the People of God "cannot err in matters of belief. This characteristic is shown in the supernatural appreciation of faith (*sensus fidei*) on the part of the whole people, when, from the bishops to the last of the faithful, they manifest a universal consent in matters of faith and morals" (CCC 92). As the *Catechism* says, "By this appreciation of the faith, aroused and sustained by the Spirit of truth, the People of God, guided by the sacred teaching authority (*Magisterium*), ... receives ... the faith, once for all delivered to the saints ... The People unfailingly adheres to this faith, penetrates it more deeply with right judgment, and applies it more fully in daily life" (93). This is the case because all the faithful—those who adhere to the Faith in mind and heart—"have received the anointing of the Holy Spirit, who instructs them and guides them into all truth" (CCC 91).

The transmission of divine revelation relies entirely upon all three legs of the stool: Apostolic (Sacred) Tradition, the sacred writings of Scripture, and the Magisterium of the Church. When any of these have been jettisoned or ignored, the Christian people have been divided by error and sin. Nevertheless, God continues to provide for the Church by sustaining her indefectibly in the power of the Holy Spirit, as the Church continues to proclaim the Word of God to all people in every generation. What makes Christianity a *living* faith is the presence of Jesus and the Holy Spirit within the Church. In the next chapter, we will explore the importance of faithful obedience to Christian discipleship. We disciples cannot merely profess the Christian Faith; we must also live it, even when it is difficult to resist the pressures of the world and even persecution. Christian faith is a long road of endurance and perseverance in hope.

18

The Obedience of Faith

The practice of *obedience* is a tough one for people today. In times past, when cultures defined social relationships according to structures of authority, law, and custom, people enjoyed relatively little personal freedom compared to what we experience here in the United States today. In fact, our experience in America is quite different from what others have experienced in most cultures around the world and throughout history. Freedom and self-determination are our cherished prizes in this country. As a result, we struggle with the idea of obedience, with those in authority telling us what to think and do. When reading Scripture, we may find it challenging, therefore, to grasp the biblical concept of the *obedience of faith*. In his Letter to the Philippians, Paul rejoices at the glory of Jesus' humility, saying, "He emptied himself, taking the form of a slave, coming in human likeness; and found human in appearance, he humbled himself, becoming obedient to death, even death on a cross" (2:6–8, NABRE). The Letter to the Hebrews expounds, "Son though [Christ] was, he learned obedience from what he suffered" (5:7–9, NABRE).

A nonbeliever might be inclined to balk at these passages. Did Jesus have any sense of his dignity and his rights? Concepts such as humility, obedience, and servitude are not easy for us to comprehend, much less practice today. As modern people, we are all about self-affirmation, self-assertion, self-determination, and self-definition of our identities in the face of social pressure and structures of conformity. Yet notice what stands at the center of all these—the self. Not the other. If in times past, Christian culture may have been too rigidly legalistic and authoritarian, today American culture has become so libertine and egocentric, it makes the gospel message of obedience to God difficult to hear and comprehend.

Our response to God's gift of salvation:
the obedience of faith

Recall that the *Catechism* states, "To obey (from the Latin *ob-audire*, to 'hear or listen to') in faith is to submit freely to the word that has been heard, because its truth is guaranteed by God, who is Truth itself. Abraham is the model of such obedience offered us by Sacred Scripture. The Virgin Mary is its most perfect embodiment" (144). The word to which we must submit freely is the Word Incarnate, Jesus Christ. The most essential truth of God's Word is that "God is love" (1 John 4:8). This is the Word that God wants us to hear, and the invitation to which he wants us, in faith, to respond. God calls all of us to submit our wills to the simple command to love God and to love our neighbor with our whole heart. "On these two commandments depend all the law and the prophets" (Matt. 22:40). Since love is the supreme act of freedom, we cannot love with divine charity unless we do so voluntarily and are willing to give ourselves to others. This is what Christian servitude is all about—nothing more, nothing less.

We noted before that Jesus calls himself "the way, and the truth, and the life" (John 14:6) and that the early Christians called themselves followers of the Way (see Acts 19:23). Christian discipleship is a path through life that is quite different from either enslavement to law (involuntary servitude) or absolute autonomy. Christianity is the path of true freedom, which we find only in the service of love. We can sum up Christian discipleship as the voluntary commitment to place one's life, in love, at the service of God and neighbor—as Jesus did. The word Scripture uses to describe this kind of love is the Greek word *agape*—or *charity*. Charity is sacrificial love. In charity, we make a gift of ourselves to others, recognizing that this is the greatest gift we can give, since God has given the same gift to each of us in Jesus Christ, his Son (see John 15:13).

In Hebrews 11, we find a great testimony to the obedience of faith, which can inspire us if we open ourselves to the mystery of obedience in love to God. The chapter begins by attesting that "faith is the realization of what is hoped for and evidence of things not seen. Because of it the ancients were well attested" (1–2, NABRE). It goes on to testify about all the examples of the obedience of faith that preceded the coming of Christ (each passage cited below is taken from the NABRE):

- By faith Abel offered to God a sacrifice greater than Cain's. (4)
- By faith Noah, warned about what was not yet seen, with reverence built an ark for the salvation of his household. (7)
- By faith Abraham obeyed when he was called to go out to a place that he was to receive as an inheritance; he went out, not knowing where he was to go.... By faith Abraham, when put to the test, offered up Isaac, and he who had received the promises was ready to offer his only son, of whom it was said, "Through Isaac descendants shall bear your name." He reasoned that God was able to raise even from the dead, and he received Isaac back as a symbol. (8, 17–19)
- By faith Moses, when he had grown up, refused to be known as the son of Pharaoh's daughter; he chose to be

ill-treated along with the people of God rather than enjoy the fleeting pleasure of sin. He considered the reproach of the Anointed greater wealth than the treasures of Egypt, for he was looking to the recompense. By faith he left Egypt, not fearing the king's fury, for he persevered as if seeing the one who is invisible. (24–27)

- Others endured mockery, scourging, even chains and imprisonment. They were stoned, sawed in two, put to death at sword's point; they went about in skins of sheep or goats, needy, afflicted, tormented. The world was not worthy of them. They wandered about in deserts and on mountains, in caves and in crevices in the earth. (37–38)
- All these died in faith. They did not receive what had been promised but saw it and greeted it from afar and acknowledged themselves to be strangers and aliens on earth, for those who speak thus show that they are seeking a homeland. If they had been thinking of the land from which they had come, they would have had opportunity to return. But now they desire a better homeland, a heavenly one. Therefore, God is not ashamed to be called their God, for he has prepared a city for them. (13–16)

Had it not been for the faith of the Old Testament saints, and had Jesus not suffered his Passion of love on the cross obediently to the Father, the promise of salvation would not have been fulfilled. Only through love and the will to make a complete gift of self in the obedience of faith did the saints of old make our salvation possible.

Mary is the exemplar of faith

When we Christians look for the perfect example of the obedience of faith, besides Jesus, we think immediately of the Blessed Virgin

Mary. Mary was the perfect embodiment of the obedience of faith. One of the stories we read in Scripture is that of the Annunciation of the Angel Gabriel to Mary (Luke 1:26–38). This moment in Mary's life is of supreme importance to the salvation of the world. Gabriel announced to Mary that God had chosen her to be the mother of the promised Messiah of Israel. It was through her that God would fulfill all his promises to save the human family. However, God's plan was a fragile one, because Mary needed to say yes. She had to accept freely this tremendous responsibility and sacrifice to receive the Word of God in her womb, to nurture and raise the child Jesus, so that eventually he could fulfill his mission to die on the cross. She had to be obedient to God's plan for her, and she had to accept freely, because God would never force her to be the Mother of his Son.

Mary answered the angel without hesitation, "Let it be to me according to your word" (Luke 1:38). Her "let it be," which the Church calls her *fiat*, changed the course of history forever and was not without tremendous sacrifice on Mary's part:

> The Virgin Mary most perfectly embodies the obedience of faith. By faith Mary welcomes the tidings and promise brought by the angel Gabriel, believing that "with God nothing will be impossible" and so giving her assent: "Behold I am the handmaid of the Lord; let it be [done] to me according to your word." Elizabeth greeted her: "Blessed is she who believed that there would be a fulfillment of what was spoken to her from the Lord." It is for this faith that all generations have called Mary blessed. (CCC 148)

Mary suffered much for believing that "with God all things are possible." To begin with, Mary had to explain how she became pregnant and trust that everything was going to be okay, even though people would not believe her. She would have to live with the social stigma of seemingly having been unfaithful to Joseph, her husband, even though she in fact had become the most faithful human person ever to live (Matt. 1:18–25).

Then Mary had to withstand the forces of evil, such as Herod, who would attempt to put her child to death. She had to flee to a foreign land to protect the Christ Child (Matt. 2:13–23). Over the course of Jesus' three-year ministry, she had to watch the leaders of Israel reject Jesus and find ways to falsely accuse him so they could have him put to death. She witnessed the people who had hailed his kingship suddenly turn into a lynch mob, crying out for his death. During his Passion, she endured all the tortures of his executioners, and then she had to watch him die the most horrible death imaginable (Luke 22–23).

As a faithful Jewish woman, Mary would have known the Scriptures and how the Messiah would suffer (as foretold in Isaiah 53), so she would have had some indication of what she would suffer by saying yes to God at the Annunciation. She embodied the fullness of the obedience of faith, because in her love, she completely trusted in God's plan, even when it seemed all was lost. "Throughout her life and until her last ordeal when Jesus her son died on the cross, Mary's faith never wavered. She never ceased to believe in the fulfillment of God's word. And so the Church venerates in Mary the purest realization of faith" (CCC 149). According to the wonder of God's plan of salvation, Mary stands in a long line of great men and women who submitted themselves to God's plan and waited on the Lord to fulfill his promises.

We are called to serve out of love

Because the love that motivates the obedience of faith is sacrificial and restorative, as opposed to selfish and grasping, and because of the nature of human sinfulness, this kind of love can often lead to our suffering and rejection—as it did for Mary and Jesus. Jesus tells us, "You will be dragged before governors and kings for my sake" (Matt. 10:18). In passages such as these, Jesus often warned His disciples that true love is not an easy road (see Matt. 5:43–48). Have you ever observed someone mocking another for being kind to a social outcast, someone deemed unworthy? Why do people make fun of kindness? The reason is this: charity requires personal sacrifice, especially for the sake of the weak and most vulnerable among us. It is easy to love people of power and influence. It is not so easy to love people who are poor and weak, or unable to repay kindness.

Jesus was tortured and executed because people could not accept his kindness and this kind of love. Today, we still struggle with charity. Some people prefer the harshness of the law, as the Pharisees and the Romans did, to the obedience of faith Jesus had toward his Father on behalf of sinners and social outcasts. Other people still prefer to be free to do as they please than to bind themselves in service to those the world deems unworthy of love and acceptance. The obedience of faith is nothing more than the humble submission of love to God and to the good of others in the name of Jesus Christ. It is the disciple's humble assent of mind and will to the truth that "God is love." As the Gospel of John proclaims, "For God so loved the world that he gave his only Son, that whoever believes in him should not perish but have eternal life. For God sent his Son into the world, not to condemn the world [by law], but that the world might be saved through him [by the obedience of faith]" (3:16–17). The Father enacted the salvation of the world through his Son's obedience in dying on the cross for sinners. The Father enacts our *personal* salvation through our obedience to his Son, who shows us the way of charity. As Jesus said at the Last Supper, "If you keep my commandments, you will abide in my love, just as I have kept my Father's commandments and abide in his love" (John 15:10).

Christian obedience is thus rooted in love for what is ultimately good and desirable — God. The fear of punishment is never an authentic motivation for the obedience of faith, although sometimes this is how faith begins. The mature Christian freely gives the assent of his mind, heart, and will to God because he loves God and believes in his promises. Christians trust that despite difficulty and hardship, obedience to divine love is always worth the sacrifice. Not only does the obedience of faith transform the world around us, it secures for us a heavenly home. The saints all attest to the fact that obedience to God is never contrary to human freedom or an offense against human dignity. It is, as Jesus tells us, the way to secure eternal life: "If any man would come after me, let him deny himself and take up his cross and follow me. For whoever would save his life will lose it, and whoever loses his life for my sake will find it" (Matt. 16:24–25).

19

God's Mercy and Justice

As is evident in the lengthy passage from Hebrews we considered in the last chapter, a disciple of Jesus must persevere in the grace of the Holy Spirit through all the trials and tribulations of this life. As part of our journey of faith, we must follow Christ's call to bear the cross of suffering in this life. Christians believe that we can bear Adam's curse of suffering and death, because we possess faith, hope, and charity. We know that our sufferings produce the spiritual maturity by which we are made worthy (capable) of eternal happiness. Jesus instructs, "Be perfect, as your heavenly Father is perfect" (Matt. 5:48). This is why Scripture also says that God will reward our efforts at holiness and virtue if we persevere to the end.

For this reason, St. John exhorts the faithful, "Look to yourselves, that you may not lose what you have worked for, *but may win a full reward.* Any one who goes ahead and does not abide in the doctrine of Christ does not have God; he who abides in the doctrine has both the Father and the Son" (2 John 1:8–9, emphasis mine). Similarly, St. Paul encourages the faithful, "*Rejoice in our sufferings,* knowing that suffering produces endurance, and endurance produces character, and character produces hope, *and hope does not disappoint us,* because God's love has been poured into our hearts through the Holy Spirit who has been given to us" (Rom. 5:3–5, emphasis mine). The virtue of hope is the disciple's weapon against the discouragement that comes with suffering and shame.

Christians thus believe that salvation is only complete once the disciple attains eternal union with God in Heaven, which is his reward for persevering during this life of struggle. The path a disciple must traverse is a path of suffering, because Jesus tells us that we cannot inherit the Kingdom of God unless we follow him (Luke 9:23). Yet his way passes *through* the cross, and then beyond it, to everlasting life. As we have seen already, the Paschal Mystery does not eliminate suffering and death. Thus, the Letter to the Hebrews says, "Let us rid ourselves of every burden and sin that clings to us and persevere in running the race that lies before us while keeping our eyes fixed on Jesus, the leader and perfecter of faith. For the sake of the joy that lay before him he endured the cross, despising its shame, and has taken his seat at the right of the throne of God" (12:1–2, NABRE). This is why the author of the letter encourages the faithful, "Endure your trials as 'discipline'; God treats you as sons. For what 'son' is there whom his father does not discipline?" (12:7, NABRE). In the same spirit, St. Paul encourages Timothy, "Aim at righteousness, godliness, faith, love, steadfastness, gentleness. Fight the good fight of the faith; take hold of the eternal life to which you were called when you made the good confession in the presence of many witnesses" (1 Tim. 6:11–12). St. Paul further compares the life of faith to a race, wherein the disciple must acquire discipline so as not to be disqualified at the end (1 Cor. 9:24–27).

Salvation in Christ

The Church believes two things, therefore, about salvation and the perseverance in the obedience of faith that it requires. First is that

Christianity does not proclaim a "wealth and health" gospel. God does not "reward" the obedience of faith with worldly possessions. God, indeed, blesses some disciples with wealth, but that is not an indication of holiness or favor in God's eyes. Ponder the words of Jesus to the rich young man: "If you would be perfect, go, sell what you possess and give to the poor, and you will have treasure in heaven; and come, follow me" (Matt. 19:21). If a disciple happens to be fortunate, Jesus invites him to use his wealth to help the needy. The life of discipleship requires an ongoing renunciation of self-centeredness and a constant striving toward maturity in Christian virtue. This does not occur automatically but takes time and endurance. Like the rich young man, many turn away sad because of worldly attachment.

Secondly, Christianity does not profess that salvation is instantaneous or guaranteed without ongoing conversion and confession of sins. Thus, St. John says,

> If we say we have fellowship with him while we walk in darkness, we lie and do not live according to the truth; but if we walk in the light, as he is in the light, then we have fellowship with one another, and the blood of Jesus his Son cleanses us from all sin. If we say we have no sin, we deceive ourselves, and the truth is not in us. If we confess our sins, he is faithful and just, and will forgive our sins and cleanse us from all unrighteousness. If we say we have not sinned, we make him a liar, and his word is not in us. (1 John 1:6–10)

In other words, one can lose his salvation by sin even after professing faith in Jesus. The reason this must be the case is that hypocrisy creates scandal and can lead others astray. Besides showing mercy, God must also be just. In his mercy, he always forgives sins as we humbly confess them — until the very end of our lives—but he does not tolerate a double life. Jesus calls every disciple to walk with integrity and honesty. This is why Jesus was so harsh toward the scribes and the Pharisees (Matt. 23). This also explains why the Church has always celebrated the sacrament of confession. As St. James exhorts, "Confess your sins to one another, and pray for one another, that you may be healed" (James 5:16).

If a disciple perseveres in faith throughout life by walking the path of ongoing conversion, not only will she remain joined to God forever, but the disciple will become a saint, and God will give her a share in the glory of Christ's resurrection. As the *Catechism* explains, "United with Christ by Baptism, believers already truly participate in the heavenly life of the risen Christ, but this life remains 'hidden with Christ in God'. . . . Nourished with his body in the Eucharist, we already belong to the Body of Christ. When we rise on the last day we 'also will appear with him in glory'" (1003). We will discuss everlasting life and resurrection in the next chapter.

Perseverance in faith is necessary

In the meantime, the expectation that the baptized Christian must persevere in the life of grace also presupposes that those who do not attain full maturity in Christ await another end. The Church teaches that the person who has not attained perfection will have to undergo some form of purification after death to complete the process of Christian maturation. The Church calls this experience *Purgatory*. Jesus speaks of this final purification after death when he explains, "As you go with your accuser before the magistrate, make an effort to settle with him on the way, lest he drag you to the judge, and the judge hand you over to the officer, and the officer put you in prison. I tell you, you will never get out till you have paid the very last copper" (Luke 12:58–59). St. Paul describes purgation by means of a helpful metaphor:

> According to the commission of God given to me, like a skilled master builder I laid a foundation, and another man is building upon it. Let each man take care how he builds upon it. For no other foundation can any one lay than that which is laid, which is Jesus Christ. Now if any one builds on the foundation with gold, silver, precious stones, wood, hay, stubble — each man's work will become manifest; for the Day will disclose it, because it will be revealed with fire, and the fire will test what sort of work each one has done. If the work which any man has built on the foundation survives, he will receive a reward. If any man's work is burned up, he will suffer loss, though he himself will be saved, but only as through fire. (1 Cor. 3:10–15)

God does not propose purification after death as a threat to us. St. Paul is acknowledging that the transformation of the human person as a new creation must be complete before one can enter fully into the blessed realm of the Kingdom of Heaven.

A helpful way to think of this is to imagine how only light can pass into the sun without change. The Spirit of God has to transform the disciple into a child of light to enter into what the Church calls the *Beatific Vision* — when we stand in God's presence and see him face-to-face. St. Paul thus says of the Christian, "For you are all sons of light and sons of the day; we are not of the night or of darkness. So then let us not sleep, as others do, but let us keep awake and be sober" (1 Thess. 5:5–6). St. Paul goes on to encourage the faithful by reminding them, "*For God has not destined us for wrath*, but to obtain salvation through our Lord Jesus Christ, who died for us so that whether we wake or sleep we might live with him. *Therefore, encourage one another and build one another up*, just as you are doing" (1 Thess. 5:9–11, emphasis mine).

The reality of Hell

Tragically, some do not persevere in faith by the graces received at baptism and through the other sacraments. Despite the great gift of new life the New Covenant offers, some people persist in the way of sin and death and so experience eternal separation from God after death. The Church calls this experience *damnation*. Damnation is not caused by God in any fatalistic manner but is self-imposed by the person who, in the end, refuses the gift of God's love. The *Catechism* explains damnation as follows:

> We cannot be united with God unless we freely choose to love him. But we cannot love God if we sin gravely against him, against our neighbor or against ourselves: "He who does not love remains in death. Anyone who hates his brother is a murderer, and you know that no murderer has eternal life abiding in him." Our Lord warns us that we shall be separated from him if we fail to meet the serious needs of the poor and the little ones who are his brethren. To die in mortal sin without repenting and accepting God's merciful love means remaining separated from him for ever *by our own free choice*. This state of *definitive self-exclusion* from communion with God and the blessed is called "hell." (1033, emphasis mine)

Jesus mentions Hell on numerous occasions. He describes it as the eternal misery that results from refusing to accept the invitation to attend the great banquet of God's Kingdom (Luke 14:12–24). Jesus also describes Hell as a fiery pit that consumes the damned. One way to think of this fire is as the love of God itself, which is God's personal judgment of sin. God's love is the rule and measure of what is acceptably admissible into his eternal presence. The glory of this love is that it keeps no company with anything other than itself. The darkness of sin has no place within the light. Thus, the soul that turns tragically, but insistently, in upon itself and refuses God's love can no more stand in the presence of God's glory (*doxa* in Greek) than the naked eye can stare straight into the sun at midday. The Letter to the Hebrews compares the judgment (justice) of divine love to the power of an earthquake and a consuming fire:

> See that you do not refuse him who is speaking. For if they did not escape when they refused him who warned them on earth, much less shall we escape if we reject him who warns from heaven. His voice then shook the earth; but now he has promised, "Yet once more I will shake not only the earth but also the heaven" ... Therefore let us be grateful for receiving a kingdom that cannot be shaken, and thus let us offer to God acceptable worship, with reverence and awe; for our God is a consuming fire. (12:25–26, 28–29)

While this is a terrifying image, the implication is that the love of God will consume the damned soul with an everlasting misery. The suffering of the damned will be their own doing (or undoing), however, since their hearts have closed to God's love and become hardened with hatred toward what is holy. Jesus uses the image of a great harvest to describe judgment: "The Son of Man will send his angels, and they will gather out of his kingdom all causes of sin and all evildoers, and throw them into the furnace of fire; there men will weep and gnash their teeth. Then the righteous will shine like the sun in the kingdom of their Father" (Matt. 13:41–43).

Many people today struggle with the idea that God judges us and that he would allow anyone to go to Hell. How can we reconcile this with God's perfect love? It is precisely because human sinfulness cannot be reconciled with perfect love. We cannot receive freely that to which we have closed our hearts. While it might be difficult to imagine how anyone could close their hearts to God's love, the tragic reality is that many people do. The Hell of the damned is not unfair but perfectly just. God will only give to us what we choose for ourselves. Again, human freedom is integral to our dignity; God will never force himself upon us. Hell is only the experience of those who have chosen to reject God's love. The perfect love of God—his glory—is thus blessedness to those perfected in love, purifying to those still in need of perfect love, and misery to those who hate God.

It is helpful to return to a rather important passage from the Old Testament if we truly wish to understand the relationship between God's mercy and justice. In it, God lays out how salvation works for the human heart and how we receive what we choose for ourselves. It is a long passage, but critically important to grasp if we want to understand properly the nature of God's judgment at the end of our lives:

> For this commandment which I command you today [to love] is not too hard for you, neither is it far off … the word is very near you; it is in your mouth and in your heart, so that you can do it. See, I have set before you today life and good, death and evil. If you obey the commandments of the Lord your God … *by loving the Lord your God,* by walking in his ways, and by keeping his commandments and his statutes and his ordinances, then you shall live and multiply, and the Lord your God will bless you…. *But if your heart turns away,* and you will not hear, but are drawn away…. I declare to you this day, that *you shall perish….* I have set before you life and death, blessing and curse; therefore choose life, that you and your descendants may live, *loving the Lord your God,* obeying his voice, and cleaving to him, for *that means life to*

you and length of days. (Deut. 30:11, 14–16, 17, 18, 19–20, emphasis mine)

To put an even finer point on it, the book of Sirach, another Old Testament book, tells us,

> Do not say, "Because of the Lord I left the right way"; for he will not do what he hates.... It was he who created man in the beginning, and he left him in the power of his own inclination. If you will, you can keep the commandments, and to act faithfully is a matter of your own choice. He has placed before you fire and water: stretch out your hand for whichever you wish. Before a man are life and death, and *whichever he chooses will be given to him.* (Sir. 15:11, 14–17, emphasis mine)

God is merciful because, while we live this life, he gives us everything we need to flourish, even the forgiveness of our sins, again, and again, and again. Yet God is also just, because he must give to us what we choose. He would violate his own goodness were he to force the human will and make us love him. In fact, God cannot do this without at the same time eliminating the possibility of our freely choosing him in love. The grace of Holy Spirit—the love of God poured into our hearts, as St. Paul tells us—is so important here, because it gives us the capacity to respond to God's invitation of everlasting communion, without, at the same time, forcing the human will. Yet this same grace also stands as our judge at the end of our lives. What have we done with all the love that God has given to us? Have we used it to love God in return, to love ourselves, and to love our neighbor? Or have we chosen rather to close our hearts and turn away from love?

People commonly ask, "If God knows that someone is going to end up in Hell, why does he create that person? Would it not rather be just for God to prevent him from ever coming to be?" The answer is the same. God could not do this without, at the same time, denying the dignity of human freedom. Every human life comes into existence by the human act of sexual intercourse. Yet even should a child be conceived under the worst of human conditions, God does not value or love that child any less. The grace of the Holy Spirit is the same for all, regardless of circumstance. The soul who is damned and the soul who perseveres have equal opportunity and access to God's grace. As the psalmist declares, "But you, Lord, are a compassionate and gracious God, slow to anger, abounding in mercy and truth" (Ps. 86:15, NABRE).

In one way or another, God gives every person the chance to say yes to his love. God is merciful. This is why Jesus says, "I, when I am lifted up from the earth [crucified and risen], will draw all men to myself" (John 12:32). How Jesus does this is not always so evident to us, but Christians believe Christ when he tells us that God gives every human person the opportunity to say yes. The *Catechism* explains the reach of God's mercy as follows:

> "Since Christ died for all, and since all men are in fact called to one and the same destiny, which is divine, we must hold that the Holy Spirit offers to all the possibility of being made partakers, in a way known to God, of the Paschal mystery." Every man who is ignorant of the Gospel of Christ and of his Church, but seeks the truth and does the will of God in accordance with his understanding of it, can be saved. It may be supposed that such persons would have *desired Baptism explicitly* if they had known its necessity.
>
> As regards *children who have died without Baptism*, the Church can only entrust them to the mercy of God, as she does in her funeral rites for them. Indeed, the great mercy of God who desires that all men should be saved, and Jesus'

tenderness toward children which caused him to say: "Let the children come to me, do not hinder them," allow us to hope that there is a way of salvation for children who have died without Baptism. All the more urgent is the Church's call not to prevent little children coming to Christ through the gift of holy Baptism. (1260–1261)

The heart that rejects God's love, therefore, has chosen differently from the humble heart how to use the gift of everlasting life.

20

Resurrection of the Dead and Life Everlasting

Besides the belief that God became man in the person of Jesus Christ, the single most important truth professed by Christians is that the Son of God suffered torture and execution, died on a cross, and rose from the dead three days later. The claim is that Jesus did not return to his former earthly existence but was raised to a state of glorification. This glorified state was unveiled briefly on top of Mount Tabor when Jesus was transfigured before Peter, James, and John. As Peter himself testified, "For we did not follow cleverly devised myths when we made known to you the power and coming of our Lord Jesus Christ, but we were eyewitnesses of his majesty. For when he received honor and glory from God the Father and the voice was borne to him by the Majestic Glory, 'This is my beloved Son, with whom I am well pleased,' we heard this voice borne from heaven, for we were with him on the holy mountain" (2 Peter 1:16–18; for the story of the Transfiguration, see Luke 9:28–36).

What Christians call the *Paschal Mystery* stands at the center of the Christian proclamation of faith. The Paschal Mystery encompasses the essential belief of Jesus' disciples — that Christ conquered death and gained for us everlasting life in Heaven. Jesus entered into the experience of human suffering and death in order to destroy the power of death over human life. He did not eliminate death, but made of it a path to eternal union with God. In the beginning, God created humankind for everlasting life. This is symbolized by the Tree of Life at the center of the Garden of Eden (Gen. 2:9). Unfortunately, the first sin separated us from God's love — as we have seen already — and brought the realities of suffering and death into the human experience. In a beautiful summary, the *Catechism* states,

> The Paschal mystery has two aspects: by his death, Christ liberates us from sin; by his Resurrection, he opens for us the way to a new life. This new life is above all justification that reinstates us in God's grace, "so that as Christ was raised from the dead by the glory of the Father, we too might walk in newness of life." Justification consists in both victory over the death caused by sin and a new participation in grace. It brings about filial adoption so that men become Christ's brethren, as Jesus himself called his disciples after his Resurrection: "Go and tell my brethren." We are brethren not by nature, but by the gift of grace, because that adoptive filiation gains us a real share in the life of the only Son, which was fully revealed in his Resurrection. (654)

What I wish to consider in this last chapter is why the Paschal Mystery is so central to the Christian Faith. I will do this by relying much on certain key (and at times long) passages of the New Testament. The point is not to prove that Jesus rose from the dead, but to explain why Jesus' death and resurrection are so important to the Christian Faith. As if everything we have discussed thus far were not enough, the resurrection is the reason why Christians refer to faith in Jesus Christ as "good news." Christianity is not just a code of ethics or a practice of life. We believe that in Christ, God has enacted a complete transformation of the human condition.

Shifting the paradigm

One of the challenges of grasping the significance of the Christian Faith today is that Christians have tended to rely too heavily upon a framework of law for explaining sin and redemption. While not erroneous, our focus on justice, debt, and the need for atonement for sin can, for modern people, obscure the deepest mystery of Christianity. One of the Church Fathers, St. Irenaeus of Lyons, used the term *recapitulation* to describe what Christ accomplished for us. The Incarnation of the Word and the Paschal Mystery of God's Son do not serve as some divine form of vindication, as though God needs retribution. Rather, God's plan entailed a project of restoration and re-creation, whereby the Father has given the human race a new opportunity to enter into the eternal life of the Trinity — what today we might call a new lease on life.

Because of human freedom, as I have explained, salvation did not happen in some magical way, or even by a simple declaration. God chose to create the conditions for the possibility of a free response of love to his invitation of love. This is how love works. He decided to renew human nature and empower it once more with the capacity for eating from the Tree of Life; that is, he desired that we be properly disposed once more to attain the grace of everlasting life in Heaven. Only God himself is capable of doing this for us. Without God's help, we remain trapped in our sinful and fallen human condition.

Another way to state this is to say that God wished to redeem humanity from within the reality of the human condition, rather than to force a solution upon us. With faith, we can perceive a profound dignity in God's approach, which far exceeds what today we might call an "enabling" approach. The Letter to the Hebrews explains the point in these words:

> Since therefore the children share in flesh and blood, he himself likewise partook of the same nature, that through

death he might destroy him who has the power of death, that is, the devil, and deliver all those who through fear of death were subject to lifelong bondage. For surely it is not angels that he is concerned but he with the descendants of Abraham. Therefore, he had to be made like his brethren in every respect, so that he might become a merciful and faithful high priest in the service of God, to make expiation for the sins of the people. For because he himself has suffered and been tempted, he is able to help those who are tempted. (2:14–18)

The consequence of sin is a form of bondage to the fear of death and a curse that establishes a habitual pattern of sin that leaves us perpetually separated from God's love. This is the curse of Adam—the curse of Original Sin.

In bearing the curse of Adam's death and going before us in faith into death, Jesus has given suffering and death a new significance. By means of his complete obedience to his Father, he opened up for us a path to eternal life with God, through the obedience of faith, which we lost in the Fall. He attained for fallen human nature a way to what Scripture calls *glory*. Glory is the blessed existence of the saints in Heaven, who now enjoy a perfect and complete union with God. Jesus conquered sin by conquering the fear of death and giving us hope that God will give to us himself and eternal life beyond sin and death. Jesus provided a way to replace our wounded and cursed humanity with his own.

Christ, the New Adam

The question is, how do Jesus' death and resurrection actually accomplish this? St. Paul anticipates this question when he says, "For as by a man came death, by a man has come also the resurrection of the dead. For as in Adam all die, so also in Christ shall all be made alive. But each in his own order: Christ the first fruits, then at his coming those who belong to Christ" (1 Cor. 15:21–23). St. Paul then goes on to explain how Christ offers to us his own glorified human nature in place of our fallen nature in Adam:

> But some one will ask, "How are the dead raised? With what kind of body do they come?" You foolish man! What you sow does not come to life unless it dies. And what you sow is not the body which is to be, but a bare kernel, perhaps of wheat or of some other grain.... So is it with the resurrection of the dead. What is sown is perishable [Jesus' humanity], what is raised is imperishable [Jesus' glorified humanity]. It is sown in dishonor, it is raised in glory. It is sown in weakness, it is raised in power. It is sown a physical body, it is raised a spiritual body. If there is a physical body, there is also a spiritual body. Thus it is written, "The first man Adam became a living being"; the last Adam became a life-giving spirit. But it is not the spiritual which is first but the physical, and then the spiritual. The first man was from the earth, a man of dust; the second man is from heaven. As was the man of dust, so are those who are of the dust; and as is the man of heaven, so are those who are of heaven. Just as we have borne the image of the man of dust, we shall also bear the image of the man of heaven. (1 Cor. 15:35–37, 42–49)

While this is a long explanation, it seems clear that St. Paul is not talking about substitutionary justice here, but a re-creation of the human race. By his obedience of faith, and his willingness to enter into death and then raise himself to glory, Jesus has transformed our old fallen nature into a new creation. He shares his renewed humanity with us through the gift of the Holy Spirit at baptism. This is why in the same passage, St. Paul emphatically asks,

"Otherwise, what do people mean by being baptized on behalf of the dead? If the dead are not raised at all, why are people baptized on their behalf?" (1 Cor. 15:29).

This process is known as *divinization*. When the Church baptizes a person (even a baby), the Church imparts to that person through the sacrament a small share of Jesus' resurrected nature. This is a pledge of the Father's desire to attain eternal union with this child of God who has been baptized into Christ. Baptism is only a *pledge*, because God invites every baptized person to mature into the full stature of Christ's humanity. How? By also being brought to share in Christ's divinity.

This is what St. Irenaeus describes when he uses the term *recapitulation*. The sacrament of baptism recapitulates the person in Christ. St. Paul explains, "For in Christ Jesus you are all sons of God, through faith. For as many of you as were baptized into Christ have put on Christ" (Gal. 3:26–27). The term *recapitulation* literally means that God has reattached the baptized to the head, who is Christ. St. Paul composed the following hymn of praise to Jesus to express this tremendous gift of love: "He is the head of the body, the church; he is the beginning, the first-born from the dead, that in everything he might be pre-eminent. For in him all the fulness of God was pleased to dwell, and through him to reconcile to himself all things, whether on earth or in heaven, making peace by the blood of his cross" (Col. 1:18–20).

The point of baptism is that it gives us an initial partaking in the eternal life that Jesus shares with the Father. This grace of the Spirit dwelling within the soul then empowers the baptized to conquer the tendency toward sin within his heart and flesh. St. Paul explains it like this: "For the law of the Spirit of life in Christ Jesus has set me free from the law of sin and death. For God has done what the law, weakened by the flesh, could not do: sending his own Son in the likeness of sinful flesh and for sin, he condemned sin in the flesh, in order that the just requirement of the law might be fulfilled in us, who walk not according to the flesh but according to the Spirit" (Rom. 8:2–4).

What can separate us from the love of God?

The key to understanding the inner transformation of the heart, however, is understanding the role that fear plays in human sinfulness. Fear cuts us off from the effects of God's love (grace) in the soul. Sin does not cause God to stop loving us in any way; sin causes us to cease to experience God's love within us. Sin replaces our knowledge of God's love with the fear of God's judgment. We impose this "separation" or "exile" from God on ourselves when we sin. St. John says, "There is no fear in love, but perfect love casts out fear. For fear has to do with punishment, and he who fears is not perfected in love" (1 John 4:18). According to Genesis, fear of punishment (that is, shame) is exactly what drove Adam and Eve into hiding in the Garden and not into the merciful arms of their Heavenly Father. Their banishment from the garden is a figurative way of explaining that Adam and Eve were no longer able to participate in the communion of God's love (Gen. 3:22–24). Thus, God no longer permitted them near the Tree of Life until he was able to restore human nature to its original innocence in Christ.

Sin and the fear of punishment bind humanity to the spiritual pathology of shame and the mistaken belief that sin makes us unworthy of God's love. Fear paralyzes the human heart and keeps us from possessing the freedom that comes with trusting in God. God's love is precisely what Satan's lie questioned (Gen. 3:1–5). Satan deceived Adam and Eve by calling into question the integrity of God's intentions toward them. Because Adam and Eve accepted this lie, fear of punishment replaced the love of God in their hearts. They experienced shame.

The historical precision of Genesis 3 is far less important than the psychology of sin and shame the text conveys. This experience of the loss of innocence is universal, since the first sin separated us all from grace. Nor can we destroy the power of shame's bondage by our own strength. Only the grace of Jesus Christ can ultimately liberate the human person from sin and death.

The basis of our hope

By experiencing suffering and death for us and rising from the dead, Jesus gives us real hope that we can attain an everlasting communion of love with God. The pledge of that union is a share in Christ's own resurrected humanity, which is a seed of everlasting life placed in the soul at baptism. This is why St. Paul declares, "Therefore, since we are justified by faith, we have peace with God through our Lord Jesus Christ. Through him we have obtained access to this grace in which we stand, and we rejoice in our hope of sharing the glory of God" (Rom. 5:1–2). In a more expanded exhortation, St. Paul explains how the power of the resurrected Christ frees the human heart from the bondage of sin, shame, and death:

> Do you not know that all of us who have been baptized into Christ Jesus were baptized into his death? We were buried therefore with him by baptism into death, so that as Christ was raised from the dead by the glory of the Father, *we too might walk in newness of life.* For if we have been united with him in a death like his, we shall certainly be united with him in a resurrection like his. *We know that our old self was crucified with him so that the sinful body might be destroyed, and we might no longer be enslaved to sin.* For he who has died is freed from sin. But if we have died with Christ [in baptism],

we believe that we will also live with him. For we know that Christ being raised from the dead will never die again; death no longer has dominion over him. The death he died he died to sin, once for all, but the life he lives he lives to God. So you also must consider yourselves dead to sin and alive to God in Christ Jesus. (Rom. 6:3–11, emphasis mine)

In effect, through baptism, Christ raises the soul to new life. Strengthened and shored up by the grace of the Holy Spirit, the christened soul is thus able to transcend the fear of death, which leads to sin and the temptation to weakness. The soul experiences the communion of love for which God made humankind in the first place. *Recapitulation*: this is the power of the New Covenant.

It is with good reason, then, that Jesus says of himself, "I am the resurrection and the life; he who believes in me, though he die, yet shall he live, and whoever lives and believes in me shall never die" (John 11:25–26). The death he speaks of here is not physical death, but the spiritual death of eternal separation from the communion of God's love. So vital is the disciple's faith in Jesus! God's plan of salvation is not magic. He does not overwrite the created order but transforms the human person through the power of the Spirit, which comes to us through the Paschal Mystery. Once baptized, Christians most connect to the power of the Paschal Mystery at the celebration of the Eucharist, when the death and resurrection of Jesus are made present. Through the Eucharist, Jesus builds up the Body of Christ and causes its maturation in the Spirit.

And I will raise him on the last day

During the Bread of Life discourse in the Gospel of John, Jesus indicates how Christians grow fully into their new lives as adopted sons and daughters of the Father. While baptism initiates us into everlasting life in Christ, it is by consuming the Eucharist that we grow into the fullness of the eternal life Jesus gives us. Jesus tells us, "Truly, truly, I say to you, unless you eat the flesh of the Son of man and drink his blood, you have no life in you; he who eats my flesh and drinks my blood has eternal life, and I will raise him up at the last day" (John 6:53–54). Thus, in a very concrete way, we consume the life we gain in Christ at the Eucharistic table. God feeds us with his body, blood, soul, and divinity. This gift in turn effects our growth in the spiritual life, by which we attain Heaven. As we assimilate the Eucharist into our bodies, Jesus assimilates us into his body — that is, into his humanity and resurrected glory. This is why, when speaking about his Eucharistic body, Jesus says, "It is the spirit that gives life, the flesh is of no avail; the words that I have spoken to you are spirit and life" (John 6:63). The flesh he is speaking about is ours, not his, while the spirit is his and not ours. The life he gives is his own — flesh and spirit.

To conclude this book, I would like to consider what has been perhaps one of the most incredible claims of the Christian Faith from its very beginning. Does the human body really rise from the dead? Can we really believe that God reunites the body with the soul? Even for the early Church, an everlasting *spiritual* existence was much easier to believe in than a bodily one. The Church has always maintained her belief in the resurrection of the body at the end of time. The fittingness of this belief rests in the fact that it makes no sense to believe that Jesus has conquered death if he has actually *not* conquered death.

Death is the separation of the soul and the body. As we discussed in the chapter on Original Sin, Christians believe that sin so weakened the soul that it could no longer preserve the body from corruption. If the body is an integral part of our humanity, then it makes perfect sense that an essential part of our redemption in Christ is experiencing the fullness of our human nature forever — except that the experience of resurrection is, as we saw above, one of glorification. The same is true for the damned — they, too, will experience their eternal misery within their bodies. Even in the early Church, the idea of bodily resurrection was so incredible that St. Paul chastised some believers for doubting it:

> Now if Christ is preached as raised from the dead, how can some of you say that there is no resurrection of the dead? But if there is no resurrection of the dead, then Christ has not been raised; if Christ has not been raised, then our preaching is in vain and your faith is in vain. We are even found to be misrepresenting God, because we testified of God that he raised Christ, whom he did not raise if it is true that the dead are not raised. For if the dead are not raised, then Christ has not been raised. If Christ has not been raised, your faith is futile and you are still in your sins. Then those who have fallen asleep in Christ have perished. If for this life only we have hoped in Christ, we are of all men most to be pitied. (1 Cor. 15:12–19)

The resurrection of the body is just one more way to emphasize the dignity of the human person and the supreme value God places on the human person — body and soul.

The human race is not, by nature, shameful. To "be a body" is an integral part of being human. Recall from the chapter on the creation of humankind that every human being is a microcosmos and thus a temple of the Holy Spirit. When the faithful rise from the dead, God will join his love to the body of the saints in a consummation of everlasting and nuptial ecstasy. The book of Revelation describes it like this: "Hallelujah! For the Lord our God the Almighty reigns. Let us rejoice and exult and give him the glory, for the marriage of the Lamb has come, and his Bride has made herself ready; it was granted her to be clothed with fine linen, bright and pure" (19:6–8).

Scripture begins with the holy marriage of Adam and Eve and ends with the holy marriage of Christ and the Church. As we saw earlier, St. Paul tells us that marriage is the sign (sacrament) of the "great mystery" of Christ's love for the Church (Eph. 5:32). St. Paul describes this great mystery as "the mystery hidden for ages and generations but now made manifest to his saints. To them God chose to make known how great among the Gentiles are the riches of the glory of this mystery, *which is Christ in you, the hope of glory*" (Col. 1:26–27, emphasis mine). Christ in you! Down through the ages of human history, God's plan has been nothing more than an everlasting nuptial union with humankind. He loves us that much. God's revelation ends with an invitation from the Church in Heaven: "The Spirit and the Bride say, 'Come.' And let him who hears say, 'Come.' And let him who is thirsty come, let him who desires take the water of life [the Holy Spirit] without price.... Amen. Come, Lord Jesus!" (Rev. 22:17, 20). The choice that God puts before every human person is this: will you say yes to the One who has loved you to the end?

About the Author

Michel Therrien is president of Preambula Group, a lay apostolate serving the work of the New Evangelization in the Diocese of Pittsburgh. He served as the president of the Institute for Pastoral Leadership in the Diocese of Pittsburgh as well as the director of evangelization. Prior to this, he served as a professor of moral theology at the Augustine Institute in Denver. He taught for seven years at St. Vincent Seminary in Latrobe, Pennsylvania, also serving as academic dean from 2008 to 2012. He holds a doctorate in fundamental moral theology from the University of Fribourg, Switzerland (2007). He and his wife, Lynn, and their four children live in Freedom, Pennsylvania.

Sophia Institute

Sophia Institute is a nonprofit institution that seeks to nurture the spiritual, moral, and cultural life of souls and to spread the Gospel of Christ in conformity with the authentic teachings of the Roman Catholic Church.

Sophia Institute Press fulfills this mission by offering translations, reprints, and new publications that afford readers a rich source of the enduring wisdom of mankind.

Sophia Institute also operates the popular online resource CatholicExchange.com. *Catholic Exchange* provides world news from a Catholic perspective as well as daily devotionals and articles that will help readers to grow in holiness and live a life consistent with the teachings of the Church.

In 2013, Sophia Institute launched Sophia Institute for Teachers to renew and rebuild Catholic culture through service to Catholic education. With the goal of nurturing the spiritual, moral, and cultural life of souls, and an abiding respect for the role and work of teachers, we strive to provide materials and programs that are at once enlightening to the mind and ennobling to the heart; faithful and complete, as well as useful and practical.

Sophia Institute gratefully recognizes the Solidarity Association for preserving and encouraging the growth of our apostolate over the course of many years. Without their generous and timely support, this book would not be in your hands.

www.SophiaInstitute.com
www.CatholicExchange.com
www.SophiaInstituteforTeachers.org

Sophia Institute Press® is a registered trademark of Sophia Institute.
Sophia Institute is a tax-exempt institution as defined by the
Internal Revenue Code, Section 501(c)(3). Tax ID 22-2548708.